Dickens' Christmas

A VICTORIAN CELEBRATION

◆ SIMON CALLOW ◆

FRANCES LINCOLN

For Ann Mitchell,
superb actress, dear friend and deeply informed Dickensian

FRANCES LINCOLN LIMITED
4 Torriano Mews
Torriano Avenue
London NW5 2RZ
www.franceslincoln.com

Dickens' Christmas
Copyright © Frances Lincoln Limited 2003
Text copyright © Simon Callow 2003
Illustrations copyright © as listed on page 160

British Library cataloguing-in-publication data
A catalogue record is available from the British Library

ISBN 0 7112 2008 5

Printed and bound in China by Kwong Fat Offset Printing Co. Ltd

2 4 6 8 9 7 5 3

ENDPAPERS: A Christmas Still Life, *Eloise Harriet,* fl. *1852–93*
TITLE PAGE: *Old Father Christmas bearing a wassail bowl*
ABOVE: *Christmas pudding, from Washington Irving's* The Sketch Book of Geoffrey Crayon, *1820*
FAR RIGHT: *Engraving of Charles Dickens, from Cedric Dickens'* Drinking with Dickens, *1983*
RIGHT: *Dickens' signature, circa 1834*

Contents

INTRODUCTION

For some time I have been appearing in a play by Peter Ackroyd called *The Mystery of Charles Dickens*. Inevitably people have asked what the mystery is, to which the reply must be: almost everything about Dickens was mysterious, not in the Agatha Christie sense, but in the sense of being unaccountable. He was one of the oddest men ever to take up a pen. And yet this egregious figure, this uncommon man, held a position in the hearts and minds of his readers, especially the working man and woman, like no other. He seemed to be writing for them; to be speaking for them, on their behalf, voicing their hopes and beliefs, celebrating their lives. And in none of his works did he do this more completely than *A Christmas Carol*, the book in which, if he didn't actually invent it, he permanently transformed the meaning of Christmas. G.K. Chesterton, who wrote some of the most perceptive commentaries on Dickens, observed that, 'the mystery of Christmas is in a manner identical with the mystery of Dickens. If ever we adequately explain the one we may adequately explain the other.'

The present book attempts if not to solve, at least to unravel those twin mysteries, first by looking at the man who wrote not only *A Christmas Carol*, but a whole series of writings for and about Christmas, and then by discovering what, in Chesterton's phrase, 'Christmas did for Dickens' – by looking at what Christmas was before Dickens wrote about it, and how he and it changed. This will involve a considerable and somewhat wandering journey, from arcane rituals of the Ancient World, through plum pudding and forfeits, carols and trees, to Christmas dinner and kissing under the mistletoe.

But it starts in the English coastal town of Portsmouth, in Hampshire.

LEFT: *A portrait of the young Charles Dickens, painting by Daniel Maclise (1806–70)*

DICKENS
the MAN

———◆◆◆———

DICKENS THE MAN

Charles Huffam Dickens was born in Landport, a suburb of Portsea (as Portsmouth was then known), on 7 February 1812. Dickens' father, John, was a clerk in the Admiralty; his parents, and theirs, had been in domestic service. A gift of mimicry ran in the blood of Dickens' family: his mother, Elizabeth – who also came from a line of domestic servants – was particularly brilliant at impersonations; she had a very sharp and not uncensorious eye and was a splendid raconteur with a special sense of pathos, often bringing her audience to tears. She loved dancing, and was very good at it.

Dickens' father's affability and generosity combined with his mother's slightly brittle vivacity to give him an enviably happy, lively childhood. He was, he later wrote, 'a child of singular abilities, quick, eager, delicate and soon hurt, bodily or mentally', an avid reader and an insatiably curious student, blessed from the age of nine with a school-teacher who encouraged and guided his almost excessively enthusiastic pupil's appetite for learning. Dickens' other great passion – for the stage – was also freely indulged; almost before he could walk he was taken to see a wide range of entertainments, from slapstick comedy to *Richard III*, while he himself would perform at the drop of a hat, singing, dancing, reciting, doing startlingly accurate impressions of local types.

The family moved briefly to London when Dickens was two years old, but they settled in leafy Chatham, in Kent, in 1816, where they stayed until 1821, when they moved back to London. Then began the upheavals which so disturbed the young Dickens, but to which we undoubtedly owe his development into a great artist. The move had been provoked by a financial crisis, one of many due to John Dickens' innate profligacy. Elizabeth Dickens attempted to open a school – 'Mrs Dickens' Establishment', she called it – but she failed to enrol a single student, while John Dickens started borrowing ever more heavily.

For Dickens, the worst aspect of the move was the loss of his education. He was in a state of high intellectual excitement when they left Chatham, on the brink of real progress, and his frustration at its interruption was intense, but his father could see no need to continue his schooling. The ten-year-old Dickens was as much hurt by his father's inability to see how desperately he needed to learn as he was by the loss of learning itself. He fell into a state

PAGES 6–7: *A London street scene, painting by J.O. Parry, 1835*

8

of dire neglect, having nothing to do but wander his filthy new city. 'I lounged about the streets insufficiently and unsatisfactorily fed,' he wrote towards the end of his life. 'I know that, but for the mercy of God, I might have been, for any care that was taken of me, a little robber or vagabond.'

He looked to his books for salvation. 'They kept alive my fancy, and my hope of something beyond that place and time.' But even that refuge was denied him when the books were pawned, going the same way as much of the furniture and effects, as his father continued to run up larger and larger debts.

The Dickenses lived in what was in effect a slum – Camden Town in north London, cramped, damp, depressing, shrouded in the smog and fog of what he called 'a great and dirty city', far removed from the countryside in which he had spent most of his early years. It must have seemed to him that nothing could be worse than his present situation, this 'descent into the poor little drudge I had been since we came to London', but there was something more terrible ahead of him. His parents triumphantly secured him a job in Warren's, a shoe blacking warehouse run by an acquaintance of theirs and, just days after his twelfth birthday, he went to work in that gloomy, rat-infested place by the Thames. Again, the distress he experienced was made infinitely worse by his parents' inability to conceive of his suffering. On the contrary, they were quite satisfied. 'They could hardly have been more so, if I had been twenty years of age, distinguished at a grammar school, and going to Cambridge . . . it is a wonder to me how I could have been so easily cast away at such an age.'

He now descended into hell, working a ten-hour day, engaged in the most menial of tasks, in the most sordid of conditions, surrounded by the roughest of working companions. He was tormented by the loss of his former happiness, and by the collapse of his dreams of growing up to be a learned and distinguished man. 'What I had learned, and thought, and delighted in, and raised my fancy and my emulation up by, was passing away from me, never to be brought back any more.'

Fate had another cruel card up its sleeve. Eleven days after the twelve-year-old boy first went to work at Warren's, his father John was arrested for debt, and sent to the Marshalsea Prison. More humiliation, more shame, to say nothing of the agony of watching a loved parent weeping openly before him. When his mother and brothers and sisters – by now five in number – went to stay with John Dickens in the prison, Dickens himself was put into lodgings. John Dickens was able to discharge himself from prison after he came into

an inheritance, but he made no attempt to remove Dickens from Warren's. As the final blow to the boy's dignity, the warehouse moved to Covent Garden, and he was put to work in the window.

One day, John Dickens walked past that window and saw his son, quickly averting his eyes. Perhaps it was this that finally persuaded him to remove the boy from employment. When he did so, it was in the teeth of fierce opposition from Dickens' mother, who could see no reason to make young Charles dependent again. He was sent to a day school – Dickens described the headmaster as 'the most ignorant man I ever met in my life' – but he snatched what education he could, indulging his passion for the theatre in school plays. The factors determining the dynamic of his psyche had been clearly established in these first thirteen years: the shock of being uprooted from the beneficent and life-enhancing atmosphere of his first ten years; the desperate attempt to recover that lost happiness and to block out the memory of the pain; the precocious awareness of suffering and injustice; great complexity in his relationship with his parents, of whom he could never be certain again. The ever-increasing energy with which he approached the world seems to have gained its impetus from the need to rise above the darkness within which at all times threatened to engulf him, and to seek affirmation in the approval and love of his public, the only source of love great enough to assuage his profound sense of rejection and betrayal.

He left school for ever at the age of fifteen; apart from dame-school and his brief sojourn at the Reverend Giles' School in Chatham, his two years at the Wellington House Classical and Commercial Academy were the only formal education he ever received. He went to work as a lawyer's clerk, spending every spare moment at the British Museum – when, that is, he wasn't walking the city, absorbing its sights and sounds and smells,

ABOVE: *An engraving showing Charles Dickens delivering some sketches by 'Boz' – his illustrationist pseudonym – to the magazine edition box of the* Morning Chronicle

assimilating its people and physical properties into his imagination, where he transformed them into the huge metaphorical shapes that fill his books. He went to the theatre every night, he claimed, for three years. No great novelist has ever been so thoroughly immersed in the theatre of his times: his plot devices, his construction of character, his command of rhetoric and his surreal sense of humour all derive directly from the theatre, an influence

ABOVE: Dickens in the Character of Sir Charles Coldstream, *painted by Augustus Egg (1816–63)*

which is felt in *A Christmas Carol* perhaps more strongly than in any of his books. It was the great dream of the young Dickens to go on stage; he even secured an audition with a West End manager, but at the last moment he cancelled it. By then his destiny as a writer was manifest.

At the age of seventeen he was taught shorthand by his father, who had begun a new career as a journalist. Dickens followed in his footsteps, and rapidly became famous as a shorthand reporter in both Houses of Parliament. He started writing, with some success, under the name of Boz (the family nickname of his baby brother), and at the age of twenty-three, he was commissioned to write the sketches which would become *The Pickwick Papers*. The monthly episodes had a slowish sale at the start, but with the invention of Sam Weller, they became a craze. When the completed novel was published in book form, it was an instant best-seller, and not just in the English-speaking world: it was immediately translated into all the great European languages, including Russian. At the age of twenty-five, Dickens was world famous.

Thereafter, his output barely flagged, though he was always prone to debilitating depressions and bouts of ill health. It is almost impossible to credit the man's productivity. Quite apart from the major novels, which, at least in the early years, were punishingly produced in monthly instalments, he wrote literally thousands of letters, all by hand; he never had a secretary. He was drawn with increasing passion to the cause of social reform, writing innumerable articles and delivering many speeches on the subject, but his concern was also expressed in direct action, sitting on many committees, and involving himself in the day-to-day running of philanthropic bodies. He founded and edited a crusading national daily paper. From 1850, he edited a monthly magazine, a great deal of which he wrote himself. He travelled extensively, to Italy, and then to America, twice – the first time in 1842, where he caused a furore by criticizing his hosts, attacking slavery, conditions

ABOVE: *Mrs Charles Dickens (Kate) in 1842*

in prisons and the corruption of political life, the
second time in 1867, after the Civil War and the
transformation of American public life, when he
was greeted rapturously.

Reading tours dominated Dickens' life
from 1858 till his farewell to the stage in
1870, the year of his death. His decision to
read publicly from his work was the result
of complex motives: from childhood he had
adored performing, and had done so in an
amateur capacity all his life. He was very
good at it; at the height of his fame, an
elderly extra told him: 'What an actor you
would have been, Mr Dickens, if it hadn't been
for them books.' But at the time of the first reading
tour, he needed to know that he still had the love of his
public. In 1858, he had abruptly separated from his wife,
creating uproar among moralists. The separation was directly connected to his secret
infatuation with an eighteen-year-old actress, Ellen Ternan, who soon became the
emotional centre of his life – his private life, that is: his real centre was to be found in his
relationship with his readers. It was this which he sought to restore by taking himself to
them in person. He also needed, or felt that he needed, to make money.

In all these objectives, he was wholly successful. He made a great deal of money; he
fulfilled his thespian aspirations ('Oh, the joy of assumption!'); and he experienced the
love of his public as never before. 'It was not applause,' said one of his listeners, 'it was
a passionate outburst of love for the man.' The very first reading was of *A Christmas
Carol*, which remained unquestionably the most popular selection over the ensuing
years; it was indeed the very last reading he gave. Physically frail, haggard, seeming very
much older than his fifty-seven years, he made an emotional curtain speech: 'From these
garish lights I vanish now forevermore with a grateful, heartfelt, respectful and
affectionate farewell.' Six months later, he was dead. 'We have lost our best friend,' a
London labourer was overheard to say. In another part of the city, a flower girl asked,
'Does this mean Father Christmas is dead?'

ABOVE: *Ellen Ternan*

THE SPIRIT
OF CHRISTMAS
PAST

The Spirit of Christmas Past

So what was the history of Christmas when Dickens transformed it? A very long and ancient one, to be sure, and not a particularly Christian one.

It might, indeed, be said that the history of Christmas has been the unequal struggle of the Christian Church to suppress its pagan heart. The notion occasionally implied by Dickens that Christmas is somehow a natural expression of the sentiments of the Sermon on the Mount is hard to sustain; in fact it is a barely modified expression of the Roman Empire and its civilization (of which Christ himself was of course a subject) and the god it celebrates is not Yahweh or his son, but Saturn.

Saturnus was identified by the Romans with an ancient god of sowing and husbandry who had presided over a Golden Age of eternal summer, when all mankind was equal, when joy and pleasure were the norm and when food was ever-abundant. The Romans believed that he had been brought to Italy by Janus, the god who looks back to the old year and forward to the new. It is striking that from the very first, the festival that became Christmas harked back to an earlier order, to an ideal dispensation in the distant past. As we shall see, this is a common theme in all stages of its evolution.

'On the first day of the Saturnalia, Saturn's own festival day,' writes the anthropologist Roderick Marshall, 'there was an outdoor banquet attended by senators and *equites* or knights – that is to say, the gentry of Rome – who laid aside their togas, if not for the animal skins believed to have been worn by Saturn and his frolicsome followers, at least for a loose-fitting and fringed gown . . . after drinking and feasting they separated with the famous cry, "Io Saturnalia!" and then for a week schoolchildren had holidays, the law courts were closed, all work was stopped, war was suspended unless the enemy insisted on attacking, and no criminals were killed or punished.' All this was an encouragement to the winter sun to revive in readiness for 'baby-faced Janus's' arrival. The Saturnalia was the part of the festival centred around the Winter Solstice, and it sought to recreate life as it was lived during the Golden Age, however temporarily. The feast lasted from 17 to 23 December. There was drinking, dancing, the giving of presents – lamps, candles, dolls and branches of evergreen.

PAGES 14–15: The Early Fruits of the Earth offered to Saturn, *painting by Giogio Vasari (1511–74)*
LEFT: *December: pig-killing and bread-baking. Illuminated manuscript from the* Golf Book of Gerhard Hoornbach, *c.1520*

17

This season of generosity, according to Libianus, writing in the 4th century, continued till Kalends, on 1 January.

> The impulse to spend seizes everyone. . .
> People are not only generous themselves,
> But also towards their fellow men.
> A stream of presents pours itself
> Out on all sides.
> The Kalends Festival banishes all that is connected with toil,
> And allows men to give themselves up to undisturbed enjoyment.

Houses and shops and public buildings all blazed with light. The normal order of things was reversed: cross-dressing was actively encouraged – women as men, men as women, and men and women as animals. Slaves were waited on by their masters; children, in Roman society normally seen but not heard, were allowed to take part. They even had a festival of their own, the Juvenilia. All – men, women, children, servants, slaves – participated in the 'dance of the god' whose purpose was to bring new life and energy to the flagging world. A mock king – Saturnalicus Princeps – was elected and had the power to command his fellows. 'One of them he might order to mix the wine,' in the words of the pioneering anthropologist Sir James Frazer, 'another to drink, another to sing, another to dance, another to speak in his own dispraise, another to carry a flute-girl on his back round the house.' These mock-kings or Lords of Misrule bear more than a passing resemblance to the figure we call Father Christmas; more of him later.

The succession of rival gods during the Roman period led to a cross-pollination of cults; the emergence of the cult of Mithras from Persia contributed other elements to the tradition which evolved into Christmas. Mithras' splendidly named Festival of the Birthday of the Unconquered Sun took place on 25 December, the day of the Winter Solstice itself; like Jesus, he was born with shepherds in attendance and had a Last Supper with his followers, he was expected to return to earth to raise the dead, and his followers believed that they had been born again to a new life. Mithras' cult to some extent overtook that of Apollo, installed in the Pantheon of gods by the Emperor Augustus, during whose reign Christ was born. Apollo replaced Sol, whose festival was also on 25 December. Nor was the significance of this date confined to Rome: Egyptian celebrants in their shrines marked the rebirth of the sun by crying out, 'The Virgin has brought forth! The light is waxing!' – personifying the new-born sun in the form of an infant, whom they then brought forth every 25 December.

All these celebrations and rituals belong to the Mediterranean and to the Near East; they were deeply embedded in the pagan culture which the Christian faith sought to replace. Sensibly, however, the early Church, rather than abolishing these traditions, allied itself to them. In the 4th century AD it was decided to hitch the celebration of Christ's birth – hitherto observed on 6 January – to the ancient Saturnalia, a development formally endorsed two centuries later by that early master of spin, Pope Gregory the Great

(AD 534–606), who was mindful of the advantages of allying the tiresomely tenacious old customs to the new theology, thus initiating an uneasy liaison between Christianity and everything it was supposed to supersede, a constant source of tension ever since.

In the sun-starved north, of course, there were different forms to the celebration of the Winter Solstice and different elements, which centred on the sense of the engulfing, all-pervading darkness of those regions and the need to use light and fire as counter-agents to the ominous gloom. The Scandinavian Yule Festival literally blazed with light, the celebrations lacking none of the festive, joyful energy of their southern counterparts. The feasting dancing and drinking were on a heroic scale, driven by the need to scare away the demons of the dark. The great god Odin himself became the Yule Demon, Julebuk, appearing in ferocious mask and horns, bringing with him gifts for the children, while a boar's head was sacrificed to Leya, goddess of love and fertility. The boar was slain because of his legendary abuse of the Sun God (curiously, in Scandinavia the animal was thought to resemble the sun, with its round face and golden bristles; boar hunts were a traditional Christmas sport). The successive waves of Viking invasions of Britain ensured that the Anglo-Saxons' somewhat tenuous grasp of their adopted Christian faith was tilted heavily towards the pagan element in the celebrations; 25 December was the first day of their calendar, so Christmas sat very comfortably in the existing framework of their lives. The Church busily set about colonizing elements of the old fertility rites for Christian purposes: evergreens, for instance, were prized by pagans as a promise of life in dead of winter, so holly became emblematic of Christ's thorns; the Yule log – formerly cut from oak – was now cut from ash as an allusion to

ABOVE: *Mithras killing the bull, Roman sculptural relief, 2nd–3rd century AD*

the baby Christ's alleged ablutions in front of an ash-wood fire.

It was the Normans, conquerors of the Anglo-Saxons in the 11th century, who coined the word 'Christ-Masse'. The feudal world entered with exceptional vigour into the celebrations, which were the highlight of the annual holiday, spread over the Twelve Days of Christmas. Monarchs sought to outdo each other in the splendour and generosity of their provisions: King John and Henry III were both renowned for the lavishness of their feasts. Richard II in the mid-15th century threw banquets lasting days at a time, once entertaining over 10,000 people. This was the hey-day of Christmas, the memory of whose splendour has haunted all subsequent celebrations. The king's munificence was echoed across the land in every fiefdom where the lord provided for his underlings. The medieval season had exactly the same social purpose as the Saturnalia: a temporary suspension of hierarchies, an affirmation of prosperity, a reward for discipline and obedience, a summoning of the spirits for the long slog till spring, a pooling of common energies, an assertion of humanity. At the same time, it was an acknowledgment of the interdependence of man and the planet on which he lived, with its cycles and seasons, an appeasement of nature. Central to these considerations were the notions of conspicuous consumption, of celebration and of liberation from constraint. It has been suggested that there was also a practical aspect to the celebrations: many of the labourers might have died in the mid-winter, had they not had an opportunity to fatten up a little over the Christmas period.

ABOVE: *January: feasting Aquarius. Illuminated manuscript, c.1423*

In the late medieval period there were striking developments. The 14th century, for example, saw the inception of the tradition of the boy bishops, where a chorister was appointed temporary Bishop, and given full powers to officiate as such; while Lords of Misrule and Lords of Christmas were given remarkable licence, of which, to the strong disapproval of many, they took full advantage.

The pagan nature of the festival was scarcely concealed, and with the Reformation, and the parallel rise of Puritanism, a conviction arose in certain quarters that because of this, Christmas should be suppressed. The Puritans denounced Christmas as 'Saturn's Masse' – two hits against it: it was both pagan (Saturn) and Catholic (the Mass). Even before the Puritans began their agitation, though, the plaintive note of the decline of the real Christmas, and the need to return to its true traditions, can be heard. This sense that Christmas represents an ancient dispensation which is somehow threatened is an insistent theme in writings about Christmas at least from the 16th century. From then to the present time, Christmas has been a sort of fabulous invalid, always seeming to be at death's door, always pulling round in time for the party.

The reason for its apparent frailty lies, ultimately, in the dissolution of the feudal system with its elaborate structures of responsibility and dependency, to which Christmas really belongs, and for which it acted as a consciously contrived safety valve, although, as we have seen, an element of nostalgia for a vanished age seems an essential part of the very idea of Christmas. In the 16th century, there were concrete grounds for this feeling. As government became more centralized, aristocrats were increasingly moving to London; both Elizabeth I and James I felt obliged to send them back home at Christmas, to look to the needs of their tenants. In the early 17th century, a group of noblemen in Norfolk and Suffolk retired to their country seats specifically to revive the old seasonal customs. In Ben Jonson's *A Christmas Masque*, presented at the Court of James I in 1625, Father Christmas – wearing a long hat and a long beard, carrying a small thick club, and supported by ten children, Misrule, Minced Pie, Carol, Gambol, Post and Pair, New Year's Gift, Mumming, Wassail and Baby Cake – laments his exclusion. 'Why, gentlemen,' he cries, 'would you have kept me out? Christmas, old Christmas, Christmas of London, and Captain Christmas? . . . I have seen the time you have wished for me, for a Merry Christmas, and now you have me, they would not let me in. . .' Later he sings:

> Now their intent is above to present,
> With all their appurtenances,
> A right Christmas as of old it was,
> To be gathered out of the dances.

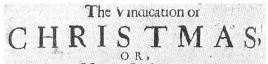

Ten years later, we find this in a chapbook:

> Christmas is my name, farre have I gone . . .
> Without regard;
> Houses where musicke was wont for to ring,
> Nothing but bats and howlets do sing. . .
> House where pleasure once did abound,
> Nought but a dogge and a shepheard is found
> Welladay!
> Place where Christmas revels did keep,
> Is now become habitations for sheepe . . .

Soon the lament would be much more urgent; Christmas was shut out for real.

In 1644, during the reign of Charles I, an Ordinance was passed banning Christmas and decreeing it a day of fasting and penance; the Ordinance originated – perhaps not entirely unexpectedly – from the Presbyterians in Scotland. It was deeply unpopular. A pamphlet from 1645 paints a pitiful picture:

A HUE AND CRY AFTER CHRISTMAS. THE ARRAIGNMENT, CONVICTION AND IMPRISONMENT OF CHRISTMAS ON ST THOMAS DAY LAST. AND HOW HE BROKE OUT OF PRISON IN THE HOLIDAYS AND GOT AWAY, ONLY LEFT HIS HOARY HAIR AND GREY BEARD, STICKING BETWEEN TWO IRON BARS OF A WINDOW.

After the execution of Charles I and the establishment of the Commonwealth, the cause of Christmas became a rallying point for the Royalists: restore the throne, they promised, and Christmas will be restored too.

And so it was; but something had gone out of it during the twelve years of the ban.

ABOVE: *A pamphlet of 1653 attacking the Puritan tax on Christmas ale. The figure in the centre represents Old Christmas*

After the Restoration, Christmas was more subdued, increasingly perceived as a thing of the past rather than the present. The years of the Commonwealth put a caesura in the national consciousness. The world was indeed changed for ever. Urban populations were swelling, the land-owning nobility were dwindling, and the 18th-century Enlightenment rejected irrational and superstitious practices, which deprived the old festival of more than a little of its vivacity. It now became a source of fascination to antiquarians, which only enhanced the sense that Christmas was something out there, distant, quaint, picturesque.

There were still vigorous survivals not only of the outward forms of Christmas, but of its properly lusty spirit. Mummers' Plays, performed at Christmas, and in which Father Christmas is frequently the central figure, were still being performed at the beginning of the 20th century. Their authenticity has been questioned, but the transcripts which pioneers started to make in the early part of the 19th century are so filled with elements we know from the Mummers' Plays of centuries earlier that it is reasonable to suppose them to have been part of a continuous oral tradition. Roderick Marshall, drawing on several of the extant plays, has reconstructed a possible opening speech for the Presenter, otherwise known as Father Christmas:

In comes I, Old Hind-before,
I comes fust to open your door.
In comes I to make the fun.
My hair is short, my beard is long. . .

ABOVE: *A 17th-century broadsheet campaigning against Christmas*

THE

TRYAL

OF

Old Father *Christmas*,

FOR

Encouraging his MAJESTY's Subjects in Idleness, Gluttony, Drunkenness, Gaming, Swearing, Rioting, and all Manner of Extravagance and Debauchery.

At the Affizes held in the

CITY of PROFUSION,

BEFORE

The Lord Chief Justice CHURCHMAN, Mr. Justice FEAST, Mr. Justice GAMBOL, and several other his Majesty's Justices of Oyer and Terminer and Goal Delivery.

By JOSIAH KING.

LONDON:

Printed and Sold by T. BOREMAN near *Child*'s Coffee-House, in St. *Paul*'s *Church-yard* ; and Sold likewise at his Shop at the *Cock* on *Ludgate-hill*.

MDCCXXXV.

Welcome or welcome not

I hope old Father Christmas will never be forgot.

Christmas comes but once a year

And when it comes, it brings good cheer,

Roast beef, plum pudding, strong ale, and mince pie,

Who likes that better than I?

I am here to laugh and cheer

And all I ask is a pocketful of money

And a cellar full of beer.

Now I have brought some gallant men with me

That will show you great activity.

Activity of youth, activity of age.

Was never such acting

Shown upon Christian stage . . .

The Father Christmas of the Mummers' Plays is enormously fat; he wears a cloak 'with pieces of wadding sewed on it' or has straw stuffed inside his coat both in front and behind, giving him the appearance of a pot-bellied hunchback. Sometimes he wears a calf's tail and carries a bladder. Often he wears a mask with whiskers which seems to have been painted red or, if he wears his own beard, the exposed portion of the mummer's face is daubed with this colour. He is always referred to as old, and announces the theme of the Mummers' Play again and again as a mystery involving 'activity of age, activity of youth'. He himself is full of vigour, and though 'just now turned into his 99 years of age . . . can hop and skip and jump like a blackbird in a cage'. Interestingly, he carries in his hand a sword, suggesting that Father Christmas had something in common with the Devil of the Miracle Play – who is after all only a demonized version of Pan, the Lord of Creation of the Ancient World, rendered diabolical by the early Church.

Of such rude and rustic survivals, the early 19th-century nostalgists were oblivious: they had a very different, roseate view of a squirearchical past, 'not a revival of medieval or feudal Christmas,' as Weightman says, 'but a re-dressing of the 18th century: a world of benevolent squires, stage-coaches, inns and ruddy-faced landlords.' Illustrations of the period have a strangely sanitized quality by comparison with the paintings of, say, Pieter Brueghel. These Georgian and early Victorian authors and painters aim to celebrate kindness

RIGHT: Pan, *painting by Sebastiano Ricci (1659–1734)*

to the disadvantaged, family cheer, general good humour, and large-scale consumption, but it is all curiously pallid. Charles Lamb has a few words on Christmas, ' . . .when mistletoe, and red-berried laurel, and soups, and sliding, and schoolboys, prevail; when the country is illuminated by fires and bright faces; and the town is radiant with laughing children'.

The American author Washington Irving is the master – and indeed, part-inventor – of this wistful genre. In his travel book *The Sketchbook of Geoffrey Crayon* (1820), he devotes Book V to Christmas, appending as epigraph a quotation from the 1645 pamphlet *Hue and Cry After Christmas*: 'But is old, old, good Christmas gone? Nothing left but the hair of his good, gray old head and beard left? Well, I will have that, seeing I can have no more of him.' In over a hundred pages, he indulges his Anglophilia – dedicated tourist that he was – consumed by nostalgia for a world and a way of life he feels he and his countrymen never knew.

He yearns for history. 'There is nothing in England,' he writes, 'that exercises a more delightful spell over my imagination, than the lingerings of the holyday customs and rural games of former times . . . they bring with them the flavour of those honest days of yore, in which, perhaps, with equal fallacy, I am apt to think the world was more home-bred, social, joyous, than at present . . . of all the old festivals, Christmas awakens the strongest and most heartfelt associations . . . There was a quaintness, too, mingled with all this revelry, that gave it a peculiar zest: it was suited to the time and place; and as the old manor house almost reeled with mirth and wassail, it seemed echoing back the joviality of long-departed days.'

Several passages from Irving's *Sketchbook* are reminiscent both of *The Pickwick Papers* and *A Christmas Carol*. Even specific phrases chime:

The dinner-time passed in this flow of innocent hilarity; and though the old hall may have resounded in its time with many a scene of broader rout and revel, yet I doubt whether it ever witnessed more honest and genuine enjoyment. How easy it is for one benevolent being to diffuse pleasure around him; and how truly is a kind heart a fountain of gladness making everything in its vicinity to freshen into smiles. The joyous disposition of the worthy squire was perfectly contagious; he was happy himself; and disposed to make all the world happy; and the little eccentricities of his humour did but season, in a manner, the sweetness of his philanthropy.

Dickens knew the book well, and echoes something of Irving's squire in his portrait of Fezziwig and in the goings-on in Dingley Dell.

'It was inspiring,' writes Irving, 'to see wild-eyed frolic and warm-hearted hospitality breaking out from amid the chills and glooms of winter, and old age throw off his apathy, catching once more the freshness of youthful enjoyment.' But sighs for the vanished yesteryear will keep breaking in. 'These fleeting customs were passing fast into oblivion, and . . . this was, perhaps, the only family in England in which the whole of them were still punctiliously observed.'

There is none of this wistfulness in Dickens. *The Pickwick Papers* bursts with vitality. There is nowhere in its pages even a hint of a dying fall. The old people have a certain nostalgia, it is true, but only for their own youths. There is no sense whatever of things coming to an end.

***

Even without Dickens, it may be noted, Christmas had grown to unprecedented popularity by the mid-19th century. Like everything else in an early 19th-century Britain still wrestling with the implications of the Industrial Revolution, Christmas was changing to accommodate new needs. There was a widespread fear that its traditions, like so many others, were being eroded and trampled under in the new conurbations, where the sense of community had disappeared, classes were sharply divided and the traditions of the agricultural communities from which so many of the new proletariat had come were abandoned and forgotten. To counter these anxieties, there was a great deal of largely celebratory writing on the subject of Christmas. In Thomas Hervey's *The Book of Christmas*, for example – published in 1836, the year *The Pickwick Papers* was first appearing in its monthly instalments, just seven years before the appearance of *A Christmas Carol* – the illustrations by Robert Seymour express pretty well everything that we think of as belonging to the Victorian Christmas; everything, that is, except the crucial element which Dickens added, his sense of the urgency of the Christmas message. Hervey and his fellow antiquarians saw it as their job to preserve a dying tradition. Curators at heart, their approach was scholarly and nostalgic.

Dickens' relationship to Christmas was quite different, nothing to do with inventing traditions and practices. For Dickens, Christmas was a living tradition, providing a unique and indispensable service for the living. His contribution was to the meaning of Christmas, and he made this contribution by the sheer force of his imagination. 'Dickens rescued Christmas not because it was historic,' as Chesterton said, 'but because it was human.'

DICKENS AND CHRISTMAS

———◆►◦◄◆———

DICKENS AND CHRISTMAS

Dickens' first writing on the subject of Christmas – 'Christmas Festivities' for *Bell's Magazine*, reprinted in *Sketches by Boz* as 'A Christmas Dinner' – was published in 1835; he was twenty-three, and was just about to start writing *The Pickwick Papers*. Both its tone and its significance immediately establish the nature of what he was subsequently to write. It has all the youthful dash of his early manner, underpinned by a sort of exasperation at those who would deny the potency of Christmas. It breathes a wholly different air from the middle-aged musings of Washington Irving. 'Christmas time!' cries the young Dickens. 'That man must be a misanthrope indeed, in whose breast something like a jovial feeling is not roused – in whose mind some pleasant associations are not awakened – by the recurrence of Christmas.' In a striking anticipation of the Cratchits' Christmas, he dares to intrude, within his very first paragraph, the darker note whose existence for him is inseparable from Christmas, and the conquest of which is a large part of the triumph of Christmas. In this way, he instinctively dramatizes the season. Out of darkness into light.

> Look on the merry faces of your children (if you have any) as they sit round the fire. One little seat may be empty; one slight form that gladdened the father's heart, and roused the mother's pride to look upon, may not be there. Dwell not upon the past; think not that one short year ago, the fair child now resolving into dust, sat before you, with the bloom of health upon its cheek, and the gaiety of infancy in its joyous eye. Reflect upon your present blessings – of which every man has many – not on your past misfortunes, of which all men have some. Fill your glass again, with a merry face and contented heart. Our life on it, but your Christmas shall be merry, and your new year a happy one!

When he thinks of the Christmas family-party – 'of which we know nothing in nature more delightful' – it is immediately and vividly in terms of dissension and rejection overcome: estranged brother and sisters reconciled, rejected daughters forgiven. Then he moves on to another great theme, that of the reunited family: 'not a mere assemblage

PAGES 28–29: Christmas Visitors, *1860, painting by William Macduff* (fl. 1844–76)
RIGHT: Merry Christmas and a Happy New Year, *cover illustration from the* Illustrated London News, *20 December 1845*

A MERRY CHRISTMAS AND A HAPPY NEW YEAR.

of relations, got up at a week or two's notice, originating this year, having no family precedent in the last, and not likely to be repeated in the next. It is an annual gathering of all the accessible members of the family.'

Due respect is paid to elders, whose foibles are indulged; children are given extreme licence, servants are swept up in the merry-making and given extra tips, hopeless young men redeem themselves with unexpectedly brilliant comic songs. There is dancing, laughing, singing, story-telling, drinking. There is turkey, plum pudding, dessert. Dickens' dancing prose summons the scene with contagious vivacity, and leaves the reader in no doubt that Christmas is in rude health and the crowning moment of the year, a season specifically devoted to the propagation of benevolence. 'Would that Christmas lasted the whole year through (as it ought), and that the prejudices and passions which deform our better nature were never called into action among those to whom they should ever be strangers!' He lauds Christmas's 'rational goodwill and cheerfulness', which, he says, do 'more to awaken the sympathies of every member of the party in behalf of his neighbour, and to perpetuate their good feeling during the ensuing year, than half the homilies that have ever been written, by half the Divines that have ever lived'.

RIGHT: Feeding the Hungry after the Lord Mayor's Banquet in Guildhall, *1882, painting by Adrian Marie*

Though personally modest in his appetite for food and drink, Dickens was powerfully in favour of sensible indulgence, and even occasional foolish indulgence. It was the symbolic significance of consumption that inspired him, the idea of happiness and relaxation and the sense of being rewarded, endorsed, cared for, cosseted, nourished which was at the heart of his celebration of these gustatory delights. To a correspondent for the Temperance League he wrote: 'In restraining Drunkards, I do not see the wisdom or the justice of depriving sober men of that which, moderately used, is undoubtedly a cheerful, social, harmless, pleasant thing – often tending to kindness of feeling and openness of heart . . . that monstrous doctrine which lays down as the consequences of Drunkenness, fifty thousand miseries which are, as all reflective persons know, and daily see, the wretched causes of it.'

Dickens, above all, believed in the common right to happiness, a thing which was often in short supply in his own life. 'Dickens devoted his genius,' wrote Chesterton, 'in a somewhat special sense to the description of happiness. No other literary man of his eminence has made this central human aim so specially his subject matter. Happiness is a mystery – generally a momentary mystery – which seldom stops long enough to submit itself to artistic observation, and joy. But here and there the note has been struck with the sudden vibration of the *vox humana*. In human tradition it has been struck chiefly in the old celebrations of Christmas. In literature it has been struck chiefly in Dickens' Christmas tales.'

Being who he was, Dickens could not conceive of a happiness which was unaware of those who were denied it. Perhaps the supreme contribution he made to the conception

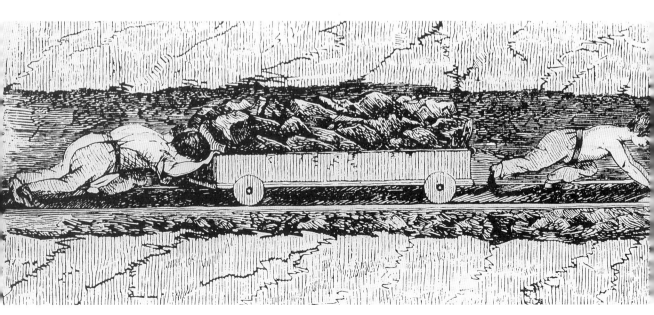

of Christmas was to focus on the disadvantaged. Of course, the great tradition of Christmas, from the Saturnalia to feudal celebrations, was the acknowledgment of the disempowered – children, servants, slaves, the poor. For this one period of the year, at least, they were to be fed and feasted; they were even briefly invested with the trappings of power. But Dickens went deeper and darker. Not only were the hard-up and the alienated to be brought into the light and the warmth: the hideous spectre which the Victorian imagination tried to block out was to be invited to the feast. As we shall see, the writing of *A Christmas Carol* sprang directly from his horror at the condition of children in employment – specifically in the mines – but even then he went further. Christmas, he insisted, was mocked unless the absolute dregs of society were rehabilitated, the root causes of their rejection and elimination from society faced and resolved.

It is a measure of the genius of Dickens, and of the power of his influence on his times, that all these disparate elements were forged into one overwhelming notion, making Christmas the point of intersection of the whole life of society, where a huge effort of benevolence, of generosity and of integration could be harnessed to heal the running wound at the heart of the world in which he lived.

BELOW: *Boys transporting coal in the mine-shafts of Lancashire*

DICKENS AND
A CHRISTMAS CAROL

Dickens and
A Christmas Carol

Dickens, like many of his contemporaries, had been moved to concern and indignation by the harrowingly illustrated 1842 Parliamentary Report on 'The Employment and Condition of Children in Mines and Manufactories'. In October of that year he and a group of friends went down the mines to investigate for themselves; his rage at what he saw knew no bounds. He planned to write a pamphlet, 'An appeal to the people of England, on behalf of the poor man's child', but while he was in Manchester in October 1843, addressing the progressive Athenaeum Club in the Free Trade Hall, an idea for a short novel came to him, and he immediately knew that this would be the 'sledge-hammer blow' he wanted to strike on behalf of the betrayed children.

It is worth noting that Dickens' speech was on a subject which never ceased to be at the heart of his concern: ignorance. The starting point of *A Christmas Carol* is neither Tiny Tim, nor Scrooge, nor the Fezziwigs' ball: it is Ignorance and Want, the causes, Dickens believes, of all the world's malaise; and the section of *A Christmas Carol* in which they are revealed from underneath his robes by the Spirit of Christmas Past is incomparably the most powerful and disturbing in the whole novel.

Dickens flung himself into the task with a focus and an energy unprecedented even for him. He had been waiting for this moment. 'I know, if I have health, I could sustain my place in the minds of thinking men, though fifty writers started up tomorrow. But how many readers do not think!' Sales of *Martin Chuzzlewit*, the book he was concurrently writing in monthly instalments, only took off when Dickens despatched his hero to America, but even then, it was not loved as its predecessors had been loved. Kate Dickens, moreover, was pregnant with their fifth child, and they were short of money. But these pressures were insignificant beside the rage to counteract the world's wickedness that propelled Dickens. He wept and laughed and wept again, he said, while he was writing the story, and 'walked about the black streets of London, fifteen and twenty miles many a night when all the sober folks had gone to beds'. He knew that what he was writing was extraordinary. When he had finished it, he underlined the words 'THE END' three times. Then, having created an ideal vision of Christmas, he hurled himself into the real one.

> Such dinings, such dancings, such conjurings, such blind-man's-bluffings, such theatre-goings, such kissings-out of old years and kissings-in of new ones . . . I broke out like a mad-man.

Dickens' exuberance was well founded: the novel was an instant best-seller. On Christmas Day 1843 it sold 6,000 copies. 'It is the greatest success, as I am told, that this ruffian and rascal has ever achieved.' Though there were sniffy reactions – 'the book does little more than promote the immense spiritual power of the Christmas turkey' – even those who were not generally disposed to praise Dickens did so. His rival William Thackeray wrote, 'Who can listen to objections regarding such a book as this? It is a national benefit and to every man and woman who reads it a personal kindness. The last two people I heard speak of it were women, neither knew the other, or the author, and both said, by way of criticism, "God bless him!"' Unconsciously echoing the last words of 'A Christmas Dinner', Lord Jeffrey declared, in the *Edinburgh Review*, that Dickens had 'done more good, and not only fostered more kindly feelings, but prompted more positive acts of beneficence, by this little publication than can be traced to all the pulpits of Christendom since Christmas 1842.' In 1871, the year after Dickens' death, Margaret Oliphant in a striking phrase recalled that '*A Christmas Carol* moved us all those days ago as if it had been a new gospel.'

The novel's effect was direct and practical: an American industrialist, having heard Dickens read from the book, closed his factories on Christmas Day; while that old curmudgeon Carlyle, according to his wife, went out and bought himself a turkey. And that was not all. 'The vision of Scrooge has so worked on [C's] nervous system that

PAGES 36–37: Scrooge's Third Visitor, *one of the original drawings for* A Christmas Carol
by John Leech (1817–64)
ABOVE: Ignorance and Want, *by John Leech*

he has been seized with a perfect convulsion of hospitality,' wrote Jane Carlyle, 'and has actually insisted on improvising two dinner parties with only a day between.'

A Christmas Carol is, above all else, about change and the possibility of change. In the words of Dickens' biographer Edgar Johnson, '[Scrooge's] conversion is a symbol of that change of heart in society on which Dickens had set his own heart.' Dickens has been criticized for making Scrooge's change of heart too abrupt, too easily accomplished. But surely that is what religion is: a sudden revelation of the right path. For Dickens, the poor were sacred, but poverty was an abomination. Only a change of heart in society at large as extreme and as lasting as Scrooge's could abolish it. Scrooge has his nose rubbed in the dirt of his life and, just in time, he is enabled to become a force for good rather than its opposite.

LEFT: The Last of the Spirits, *by John Leech*
ABOVE: Scrooge Extinguishes the First of the Three Spirits, *by John Leech*

A CHRISTMAS CAROL

IN PROSE:

BEING A GHOST STORY

OF CHRISTMAS

BY

CHARLES DICKENS

a Christmas Carol
In Prose;
Being a Short Story of Christmas.
By Charles Dickens

The Illustrations by John Leech

Chapman and Hall 186 Strand
MDCCC XL III.

I have endeavoured in this Ghostly little book, to raise the Ghost of
an Idea, which shall not put my readers out of humour with themselves, with each other,
with the season, or with me. May it haunt their houses pleasantly, and no one wish to lay it.
Their faithful friend and servant,

C. D.

December 1843

PAGES 42–43: Marley's Ghost, *by John Leech*

STAVE 1

Marley's Ghost

Marley was dead: to begin with. There is no doubt whatever about that. The register of his burial was signed by the clergyman, the clerk, the undertaker, and the chief mourner. Scrooge signed it: and Scrooge's name was good upon Change, for anything he chose to put his hand to. Old Marley was as dead as a door-nail.

Mind! I don't mean to say that I know, of my own knowledge, what there is particularly dead about a door-nail. I might have been inclined, myself, to regard a coffin-nail as the deadest piece of ironmongery in the trade. But the wisdom of our ancestors is in the simile; and my unhallowed hands shall not disturb it, or the Country's done for. You will therefore permit me to repeat, emphatically, that Marley was as dead as a door-nail.

Scrooge knew he was dead? Of course he did. How could it be otherwise? Scrooge and he were partners for I don't know how many years. Scrooge was his sole executor, his sole administrator, his sole assign, his sole residuary legatee, his sole friend and sole mourner. And even Scrooge was not so dreadfully cut up by the sad event, but that he was an excellent man of business on the very day of the funeral, and solemnised it with an undoubted bargain.

The mention of Marley's funeral brings me back to the point I started from. There is no doubt that Marley was dead. This must be distinctly understood, or nothing wonderful can come of the story I am going to relate. If we were not perfectly convinced that Hamlet's Father died before the play began, there would be nothing more remarkable in his taking a stroll at night, in an easterly wind, upon his own ramparts, than there would be in any other middle-aged gentleman rashly turning out after dark in a breezy spot – say Saint Paul's Churchyard for instance literally to astonish his son's weak mind.

Scrooge never painted out Old Marley's name. There it stood, years afterwards, above the warehouse door: Scrooge and Marley. The firm was known as Scrooge and Marley. Sometimes people new to the business called Scrooge Scrooge, and sometimes Marley, but he answered to both names: it was all the same to him.

Oh! But he was a tight-fisted hand at the grindstone, Scrooge! a squeezing, wrenching, grasping, scraping, clutching, covetous, old sinner! Hard and sharp as flint, from which no steel had ever struck out generous fire; secret, and self-contained, and solitary as an oyster. The cold within him froze his old features, nipped his pointed nose, shrivelled his cheek, stiffened his gait; made his eyes red, his thin lips blue; and spoke out shrewdly in his grating voice. A frosty rime was on his head, and on his eyebrows, and his wiry chin. He carried his own low temperature always about with him; he iced his office in the dog-days; and didn't thaw it one degree at Christmas.

External heat and cold had little influence on Scrooge. No warmth could warm, no wintry weather chill him. No wind that blew was bitterer than he, no falling snow was more intent upon its purpose, no pelting rain less open to entreaty. Foul weather didn't know where to have him. The heaviest rain, and snow, and hail, and sleet, could boast of the advantage over him in only one respect. They often 'came down' handsomely, and Scrooge never did.

Nobody ever stopped him in the street to say, with gladsome looks, 'My dear Scrooge, how are you? when will you come to see me?' No beggars implored him to bestow a trifle, no children asked him what it was o'clock, no man or woman ever once in all his life inquired the way to such and such a place, of Scrooge. Even the blindmen's dogs appeared to know him; and when they saw him coming on, would tug their owners into doorways and up courts; and then would wag their tails as though they said, 'no eye at all is better than an evil eye, dark master!'

But what did Scrooge care? It was the very thing he liked. To edge his way along the crowded paths of life, warning all human sympathy to keep its distance, was what the knowing ones call 'nuts' to Scrooge.

Once upon a time – of all the good days in the year, on Christmas Eve – old Scrooge sat busy in his counting-house. It was cold, bleak, biting weather: foggy withal: and he could hear the people in the court outside go wheezing up and down, beating their hands upon their breasts, and stamping their feet upon the pavement-stones to warm them. The city clocks had only just gone three, but it was quite dark already: it had not been light all day: and candles were flaring in the windows of the neighbouring offices, like ruddy smears upon the palpable brown air. The fog came pouring in at every chink and keyhole, and was so dense without, that although the court was of the narrowest, the houses opposite were mere phantoms. To see the dingy cloud come drooping down, obscuring everything, one might have thought that Nature lived hard by, and was brewing on a large scale.

The door of Scrooge's counting-house was open that he might keep his eye upon his clerk, who in a dismal little cell beyond, a sort of tank, was copying letters. Scrooge had a very small fire, but the clerk's fire was so very much smaller that it looked like one coal. But he couldn't replenish it, for Scrooge kept the coal-box in his own room; and so surely as the clerk came in with the shovel, the master predicted that it would be necessary for them to part. Wherefore the clerk put on his white comforter, and tried to warm himself at the candle; in which effort, not being a man of a strong imagination, he failed.

'A merry Christmas, uncle! God save you!' cried a cheerful voice. It was the voice of Scrooge's nephew, who came upon him so quickly that this was the first intimation he had of his approach.

'Bah!' said Scrooge, 'Humbug!'

He had so heated himself with rapid walking in the fog and frost, this nephew of Scrooge's, that he was all in a glow; his face was ruddy and handsome; his eyes sparkled, and his breath smoked again.

'Christmas a humbug, uncle!' said Scrooge's nephew. 'You don't mean that, I am sure?'

'I do,' said Scrooge. 'Merry Christmas! What right have you to be merry? what reason have you to be merry? You're poor enough.'

'Come, then,' returned the nephew gaily. 'What right have you to be dismal? what reason have you to be morose? You're rich enough.'

Scrooge having no better answer ready on the spur of the moment, said 'Bah!' again; and followed it up with 'Humbug.'

'Don't be cross, uncle,' said the nephew.

'What else can I be,' returned the uncle, 'when I live in such a world of fools as this? Merry Christmas! Out upon merry Christmas! What's Christmas time to you but a time for paying bills without money; a time for finding yourself a year older, and not an hour richer; a time for balancing your books and having every item in 'em through a round dozen of months presented dead against you? If I could work my will,' said Scrooge indignantly, 'every idiot who goes about with "Merry Christmas," on his lips, should be boiled with his own pudding, and buried with a stake of holly through his heart. He should!'

'Uncle!' pleaded the nephew.

'Nephew!' returned the uncle, sternly, 'keep Christmas in your own way, and let me keep it in mine.'

'Keep it!' repeated Scrooge's nephew. 'But you don't keep it.'

'Let me leave it alone, then,' said Scrooge. 'Much good may it do you! Much good it has ever done you!'

'There are many things from which I might have derived good, by which I have not profited, I dare say,' returned the nephew. 'Christmas among the rest. But I am sure I have always thought of Christmas time, when it has come round – apart from the veneration due to its sacred name and origin, if anything belonging to it can be apart from that – as a good time: a kind, forgiving, charitable, pleasant time: the only time I know of, in the long calendar of the year, when men and women seem by one consent to open their shut-up hearts freely, and to think of people below them as if they really were fellow-passengers to the grave, and not another race of creatures bound on other journeys. And therefore, uncle, though it has never put a scrap of gold or silver in my pocket, I believe that it *has* done me good, and *will* do me good; and I say, God bless it!'

The clerk in the tank involuntarily applauded: becoming immediately sensible of the impropriety, he poked the fire, and extinguished the last frail spark for ever.

'Let me hear another sound from *you*,' said Scrooge, 'and you'll keep your Christmas by losing your situation! You're quite a powerful speaker, sir,' he added, turning to his nephew. 'I wonder you don't go into Parliament.'

'Don't be angry, uncle. Come! Dine with us to-morrow.'

Scrooge said that he would see him – yes, indeed he did. He went the whole length of the expression, and said that he would see him in that extremity first.

'But why?' cried Scrooge's nephew. 'Why?'

'Why did you get married?' said Scrooge.

'Because I fell in love.'

'Because you fell in love!' growled Scrooge, as if that were the only one thing in the world more ridiculous than a merry Christmas. 'Good afternoon!'

'Nay, uncle, but you never came to see me before that happened. Why give it as a reason for not coming now?'

'Good afternoon,' said Scrooge.

'I want nothing from you; I ask nothing of you; why cannot we be friends?'

'Good afternoon,' said Scrooge.

'I am sorry, with all my heart, to find you so resolute. We have never had any quarrel, to which I have been a party. But I have made the trial in homage to Christmas, and I'll keep my Christmas humour to the last. So A Merry Christmas, uncle!'

'Good afternoon!' said Scrooge.

'And A Happy New Year!'

'Good afternoon!' said Scrooge.

His nephew left the room without an angry word, notwithstanding. He stopped at the outer door to bestow the greetings of the season on the clerk, who, cold as he was, was warmer than Scrooge; for he returned them cordially.

'There's another fellow,' muttered Scrooge; who overheard him: 'my clerk, with fifteen shillings a-week, and a wife and family, talking about a merry Christmas. I'll retire to Bedlam.'

This lunatic, in letting Scrooge's nephew out, had let two other people in. They were portly gentlemen, pleasant to behold, and now stood, with their hats off, in Scrooge's office. They had books and papers in their hands, and bowed to him.

'Scrooge and Marley's, I believe,' said one of the gentlemen, referring to his list. 'Have I the pleasure of addressing Mr. Scrooge, or Mr. Marley?'

'Mr. Marley has been dead these seven years,' Scrooge replied. 'He died seven years ago, this very night.'

'We have no doubt his liberality is well represented by his surviving partner,' said the gentleman, presenting his credentials.

It certainly was; for they had been two kindred spirits. At the ominous word 'liberality,' Scrooge frowned, and shook his head, and handed the credentials back.

'At this festive season of the year, Mr. Scrooge,' said the gentleman, taking up a pen, 'it is more than usually desirable that we should make some slight provision for the poor and destitute, who suffer greatly at the present time. Many thousands are in want of common necessaries; hundreds of thousands are in want of common comforts, sir.'

'Are there no prisons?' asked Scrooge.

'Plenty of prisons,' said the gentleman, laying down the pen again.

'And the Union workhouses?' demanded Scrooge. 'Are they still in operation?'

'They are. Still,' returned the gentleman, 'I wish I could say they were not.'

'The Treadmill and the Poor Law are in full vigour, then?' said Scrooge.

'Both very busy, sir.'

'Oh! I was afraid, from what you said at first, that something had occurred to stop them in their useful course,' said Scrooge. 'I'm very glad to hear it.'

'Under the impression that they scarcely furnish Christian cheer of mind or body to the multitude,' returned the gentleman, 'a few of us are endeavouring to raise a fund to buy the Poor some meat and drink, and means of warmth. We choose this time, because it is a time, of all others, when Want is keenly felt, and Abundance rejoices. What shall I put you down for?'

'Nothing!' Scrooge replied.

'You wish to be anonymous?'

'I wish to be left alone,' said Scrooge. 'Since you ask me what I wish, gentlemen, that is my answer. I don't make merry myself at Christmas and I can't afford to make idle people merry. I help to support the establishments I have mentioned: they cost enough: and those who are badly off must go there.'

'Many can't go there; and many would rather die.'

'If they would rather die,' said Scrooge, 'they had better do it, and decrease the surplus population. Besides – excuse me – I don't know that.'

'But you might know it,' observed the gentleman.

'It's not my business,' Scrooge returned. 'It's enough for a man to understand his own business, and not to interfere with other people's. Mine occupies me constantly. Good afternoon, gentlemen!'

Seeing clearly that it would be useless to pursue their point, the gentlemen withdrew. Scrooge resumed his labours with an improved opinion of himself, and in a more facetious temper than was usual with him.

Meanwhile the fog and darkness thickened so, that people ran about with flaring links, proffering their services to go before horses in carriages, and conduct them on their way. The ancient tower of a church, whose gruff old bell was always peeping slily down at Scrooge out of a gothic window in the wall, became invisible, and struck the hours and quarters in the clouds, with tremulous vibrations afterwards, as if its teeth were chattering in its frozen head up there. The cold became intense. In the main street, at the corner of the court, some labourers were repairing the gas-pipes, and had lighted a great fire in a brazier, round which a party of ragged men and boys were gathered: warming their hands and winking their eyes before the blaze in rapture. The water-plug being left in solitude, its overflowings sullenly congealed, and turned to misanthropic ice. The brightness of the shops where holly sprigs and berries crackled in the lamp-heat of the windows, made pale faces ruddy as they passed. Poulterers' and grocers' trades became a splendid joke: a glorious pageant, with which it was next to impossible to believe that such dull principles as bargain and sale had anything to do. The Lord Mayor, in the stronghold of the mighty Mansion House, gave orders to his fifty cooks and butlers to keep Christmas as a Lord Mayor's household should; and even the little tailor, whom he had fined five shillings on the previous Monday for being drunk and blood-thirsty in the streets, stirred up to-morrow's pudding in his garret, while his lean wife and the baby sallied out to buy the beef.

Foggier yet, and colder! Piercing, searching, biting cold. If the good Saint Dunstan had but nipped the Evil Spirit's nose with a touch of such weather as that, instead of using his familiar weapons, then indeed he would have roared to lusty purpose. The owner of one scant young nose, gnawed and mumbled by the hungry cold as bones are gnawed by dogs, stooped down at Scrooge's keyhole to regale him with a Christmas carol: but at the first sound of—

'God bless you merry gentleman!
May nothing you dismay!'

Scrooge seized the ruler with such energy of action, that the singer fled in terror, leaving the keyhole to the fog and even more congenial frost.

At length the hour of shutting up the counting-house arrived. With an ill-will Scrooge dismounted from his stool, and tacitly admitted the fact to the expectant clerk in the Tank, who instantly snuffed his candle out, and put on his hat.

'You'll want all day to-morrow, I suppose?' said Scrooge.

'If quite convenient, sir.'

'It's not convenient,' said Scrooge, 'and it's not fair. If I was to stop half-a-crown for it, you'd think yourself ill-used, I'll be bound?'

The clerk smiled faintly.

'And yet,' said Scrooge, 'you don't think *me* ill used, when I pay a day's wages for no work.'

The clerk observed that it was only once a year.

'A poor excuse for picking a man's pocket every twenty-fifth of December!' said Scrooge, buttoning his great-coat to the chin. 'But I suppose you must have the whole day. Be here all the earlier next morning!'

The clerk promised that he would; and Scrooge walked out with a growl. The office was closed in a twinkling, and the clerk, with the long ends of his white comforter dangling below his waist (for he boasted no great-coat), went down a slide on Cornhill, at the end of a lane of boys, twenty times, in honour of its being Christmas-eve, and then ran home to Camden Town as hard as he could pelt, to play at blindman's-buff.

Scrooge took his melancholy dinner in his usual melancholy tavern; and having read all the newspapers, and beguiled the rest of the evening with his banker's-book, went home to bed. He lived in chambers which had once belonged to his deceased partner. They were a gloomy suite of rooms, in a lowering pile of building up a yard, where it had so little business to be, that one could scarcely help fancying it must have run there when it was a young house, playing at hide-and-seek with other houses, and forgotten the way out again. It was old enough now, and dreary enough, for nobody lived in it but Scrooge, the other rooms being all let out as offices. The yard was so dark that even Scrooge, who knew its every stone, was fain to grope with his hands. The fog and frost so hung about the black old gateway of the house, that it seemed as if the Genius of the Weather sat in mournful meditation on the threshold.

Now, it is a fact, that there was nothing at all particular about the knocker on the door, except that it was very large. It is also a fact, that Scrooge had seen it night and morning during his whole residence in that place; also that Scrooge had as little of what is called fancy about him as any man in the City of London, even including – which is a bold word – the corporation, aldermen, and livery. Let it also be borne in mind that Scrooge had not bestowed one thought on Marley, since his last mention of his seven-years' dead partner that afternoon. And then let any man explain to me, if he can, how it happened that Scrooge, having his key in the lock of the door, saw in the knocker, without its undergoing any intermediate process of change: not a knocker, but Marley's face.

Marley's face. It was not in impenetrable shadow as the other objects in the yard were, but had a dismal light about it, like a bad lobster in a dark cellar. It was not angry or ferocious, but looked at Scrooge as Marley used to look: with ghostly spectacles turned up on its ghostly forehead. The hair was curiously stirred, as if by breath or hot-air; and though the eyes were wide open, they were perfectly motionless.

That, and its livid colour, made it horrible; but its horror seemed to be in spite of the face and beyond its control, rather than a part of its own expression.

As Scrooge looked fixedly at this phenomenon, it was a knocker again.

To say that he was not startled, or that his blood was not conscious of a terrible sensation to which it had been a stranger from infancy, would be untrue. But he put his hand upon the key he had relinquished, turned it sturdily, walked in, and lighted his candle.

He *did* pause, with a moment's irresolution, before he shut the door; and he *did* look cautiously behind it first, as if he half-expected to be terrified with the sight of Marley's pigtail sticking out into the hall. But there was nothing on the back of the door, except the screws and nuts that held the knocker on; so he said 'Pooh, pooh!' and closed it with a bang.

The sound resounded through the house like thunder. Every room above, and every cask in the wine-merchant's cellars below, appeared to have a separate peal of echoes of its own. Scrooge was not a man to be frightened by echoes. He fastened the door, and walked across the hall, and up the stairs: slowly too: trimming his candle as he went.

You may talk vaguely about driving a coach-and-six up a good old flight of stairs, or through a bad young Act of Parliament; but I mean to say you might have got a hearse up that staircase, and taken it broadwise, with the splinter-bar towards the wall, and the door towards the balustrades: and done it easy. There was plenty of width for that, and room to spare; which is perhaps the reason why Scrooge thought he saw a locomotive hearse going on before him in the gloom. Half a dozen gas-lamps out of the street wouldn't have lighted the entry too well, so you may suppose that it was pretty dark with Scrooge's dip.

Up Scrooge went, not caring a button for that: darkness is cheap, and Scrooge liked it. But before he shut his heavy door, he walked through his rooms to see that all was right. He had just enough recollection of the face to desire to do that.

Sitting-room, bed-room, lumber-room. All as they should be. Nobody under the table, nobody under the sofa; a small fire in the grate; spoon and basin ready; and the little saucepan of gruel (Scrooge had a cold in his head) upon the hob. Nobody under the bed; nobody in the closet; nobody in his dressing-gown, which was hanging up in a suspicious attitude against the wall. Lumber-room as usual. Old fire-guard, old shoes, two fish-baskets, washing-stand on three legs, and a poker.

Quite satisfied, he closed his door, and locked himself in; double-locked himself in, which was not his custom. Thus secured against surprise, he took off his cravat; put on his dressing-gown and slippers, and his night-cap; and sat down before the fire to take his gruel.

It was a very low fire indeed; nothing on such a bitter night. He was obliged to sit close to it, and brood over it, before he could extract the least sensation of warmth from such a handful of fuel. The fireplace was an old one, built by some Dutch merchant long ago, and paved all round with quaint Dutch tiles, designed to illustrate the Scriptures. There were Cains and Abels, Pharaoh's daughters, Queens of Sheba, Angelic messengers descending through the air on clouds like feather-beds, Abrahams, Belshazzars, Apostles putting off to sea in butter-boats, hundreds of figures to attract his thoughts; and yet that face of Marley, seven years dead, came like the ancient Prophet's rod, and swallowed up the whole. If each smooth tile had been a blank at first, with power to shape some picture on its surface from the disjointed fragments of his thoughts, there would have been a copy of old Marley's head on every one.

'Humbug!' said Scrooge; and walked across the room.

After several turns, he sat down again. As he threw his head back in the chair, his glance happened to rest upon a bell, a disused bell, that hung in the room, and communicated for some purpose now forgotten with a chamber in the highest story of the building. It was with great astonishment, and with a strange, inexplicable dread, that as he looked, he saw this bell begin to swing. It swung so softly in the outset that it scarcely made a sound; but soon it rang out loudly, and so did every bell in the house.

This might have lasted half a minute, or a minute, but it seemed an hour. The bells ceased as they had begun, together. They were succeeded by a clanking noise, deep down below; as if some person were dragging a heavy chain over the casks in the wine merchant's cellar. Scrooge then remembered to have heard that ghosts in haunted houses were described as dragging chains.

The cellar-door flew open with a booming sound, and then he heard the noise much louder, on the floors below; then coming up the stairs; then coming straight towards his door.

'It's humbug still!' said Scrooge. 'I won't believe it.'

His colour changed though, when, without a pause, it came on through the heavy door, and passed into the room before his eyes. Upon its coming in, the dying flame leaped up, as though it cried 'I know him! Marley's Ghost!' and fell again.

The same face: the very same. Marley in his pig-tail, usual waistcoat, tights, and boots; the tassels on the latter bristling, like his pigtail, and his coat-skirts, and the hair upon his head. The chain he drew was clasped about his middle. It was long, and wound about him like a tail; and it was made (for Scrooge observed it closely) of cash-boxes, keys, padlocks, ledgers, deeds, and heavy purses wrought in steel. His body was transparent: so that Scrooge, observing him, and looking through his waistcoat, could see the two buttons on his coat behind.

Scrooge had often heard it said that Marley had no bowels, but he had never believed it until now.

No, nor did he believe it even now. Though he looked the phantom through and through, and saw it standing before him; though he felt the chilling influence of its death-cold eyes; and marked the very texture of the folded kerchief bound about its head and chin, which wrapper he had not observed before: he was still incredulous, and fought against his senses.

'How now!' said Scrooge, caustic and cold as ever. 'What do you want with me?'

'Much!' – Marley's voice, no doubt about it.

'Who are you?'

'Ask me who I *was*.'

'Who *were* you then?' said Scrooge, raising his voice. 'You're particular – for a shade.' He was going to say '*to* a shade,' but substituted this, as more appropriate.

'In life I was your partner, Jacob Marley.'

'Can you – can you sit down?' asked Scrooge, looking doubtfully at him.

'I can.'

'Do it, then.'

Scrooge asked the question, because he didn't know whether a ghost so transparent might find himself in a condition to take a chair; and felt that in the event of its being impossible, it might involve the necessity of an embarrassing explanation. But the ghost sat down on the opposite side of the fireplace, as if he were quite used to it.

'You don't believe in me,' observed the Ghost.

'I don't,' said Scrooge.

'What evidence would you have of my reality, beyond that of your senses?'

'I don't know,' said Scrooge.

'Why do you doubt your senses?'

'Because,' said Scrooge, 'a little thing affects them. A slight disorder of the stomach makes them cheats. You may be an undigested bit of beef, a blot of mustard, a crumb of cheese, a fragment of an underdone potato. There's more of gravy than of grave about you, whatever you are!'

Scrooge was not much in the habit of cracking jokes, nor did he feel, in his heart, by any means waggish then. The truth is, that he tried to be smart, as a means of distracting his own attention, and keeping down his terror; for the spectre's voice disturbed the very marrow in his bones.

To sit, staring at those fixed, glazed eyes, in silence for a moment, would play, Scrooge felt, the very deuce with him. There was something very awful, too, in the spectre's being provided with an infernal atmosphere of its own. Scrooge could not feel it himself, but this was clearly the case; for though the Ghost sat perfectly motionless, its hair, and skirts, and tassels, were still agitated as by the hot vapour from an oven.

'You see this toothpick?' said Scrooge, returning quickly to the charge, for the reason just assigned; and wishing, though it were only for a second, to divert the vision's stony gaze from himself.

'I do,' replied the Ghost.

'You are not looking at it,' said Scrooge.

'But I see it,' said the Ghost, 'notwithstanding.'

'Well!' returned Scrooge, 'I have but to swallow this, and be for the rest of my days persecuted by a legion of goblins, all of my own creation. Humbug, I tell you – humbug!'

At this, the spirit raised a frightful cry, and shook its chain with such a dismal and appalling noise, that Scrooge held on tight to his chair, to save himself from falling in a swoon. But how much greater was his horror, when the phantom taking off the bandage round its head, as if it were too warm to wear in-doors, its lower jaw dropped down upon its breast!

Scrooge fell upon his knees, and clasped his hands before his face.

'Mercy!' he said. 'Dreadful apparition, why do you trouble me?'

'Man of the worldly mind!' replied the Ghost, 'do you believe in me or not?'

'I do,' said Scrooge. 'I must. But why do spirits walk the earth, and why do they come to me?'

'It is required of every man,' the Ghost returned, 'that the spirit within him should walk abroad among his fellowmen, and travel far and wide; and if that spirit goes not forth in life, it is condemned to do so after death. It is doomed to wander through the world – oh, woe is me! – and witness what it cannot share, but might have shared on earth, and turned to happiness!'

Again the spectre raised a cry, and shook its chain and wrung its shadowy hands.

'You are fettered,' said Scrooge, trembling. 'Tell me why?'

'I wear the chain I forged in life,' replied the Ghost. 'I made it link by link, and yard by yard; I girded it on of my own free will, and of my own free will I wore it. Is its pattern strange to *you*?'

Scrooge trembled more and more.

'Or would you know,' pursued the Ghost, 'the weight and length of the strong coil you bear yourself? It was full as heavy and as long as this, seven Christmas Eves ago. You have laboured on it, since. It is a ponderous chain!'

Scrooge glanced about him on the floor, in the expectation of finding himself surrounded by some fifty or sixty fathoms of iron cable: but he could see nothing.

'Jacob,' he said, imploringly. 'Old Jacob Marley, tell me more. Speak comfort to me, Jacob.'

'I have none to give,' the Ghost replied. 'It comes from other regions, Ebenezer Scrooge, and is conveyed by other ministers, to other kinds of men. Nor can I tell you what I would. A very little more, is all permitted to me. I cannot rest, I cannot stay, I cannot linger anywhere. My spirit never walked beyond our counting-house – mark me! – in life my spirit never roved beyond the narrow limits of our money-changing hole; and weary journeys lie before me!'

It was a habit with Scrooge, whenever he became thoughtful, to put his hands in his breeches pockets. Pondering on what the Ghost had said, he did so now, but without lifting up his eyes, or getting off his knees.

'You must have been very slow about it, Jacob,' Scrooge observed, in a business-like manner, though with humility and deference.

'Slow!' the Ghost repeated.

'Seven years dead,' mused Scrooge. 'And travelling all the time?'

'The whole time,' said the Ghost. 'No rest, no peace. Incessant torture of remorse.'

'You travel fast?' said Scrooge.

'On the wings of the wind,' replied the Ghost.

'You might have got over a great quantity of ground in seven years,' said Scrooge.

The Ghost, on hearing this, set up another cry, and clanked its chain so hideously in the dead silence of the night, that the Ward would have been justified in indicting it for a nuisance.

'Oh! captive, bound, and double-ironed,' cried the phantom, 'not to know, that ages of incessant labour, by immortal creatures, for this earth must pass into eternity before the good of which it is susceptible is all developed. Not to know that any Christian spirit working kindly in its little sphere, whatever it may be, will find its mortal life too short for its vast means of usefulness. Not to know that no space of regret can make amends for one life's opportunity misused! Yet such was I! Oh! such was I!'

'But you were always a good man of business, Jacob,' faltered Scrooge, who now began to apply this to himself.

'Business!' cried the Ghost, wringing its hands again. 'Mankind was my business. The common welfare was my business; charity, mercy, forbearance, and benevolence, were, all, my business. The dealings of my trade were but a drop of water in the comprehensive ocean of my business!'

It held up its chain at arm's length, as if that were the cause of all its unavailing grief, and flung it heavily upon the ground again.

'At this time of the rolling year,' the spectre said, 'I suffer most. Why did I walk through crowds of fellow-beings with my eyes turned down, and never raise them to that blessed Star which led the Wise Men to a poor abode? Were there no poor homes to which its light would have conducted *me*!'

Scrooge was very much dismayed to hear the spectre going on at this rate, and began to quake exceedingly.

'Hear me!' cried the Ghost. 'My time is nearly gone.'

'I will,' said Scrooge. 'But don't be hard upon me! Don't be flowery, Jacob! Pray!'

'How it is that I appear before you in a shape that you can see, I may not tell. I have sat invisible beside you many and many a day.'

It was not an agreeable idea. Scrooge shivered, and wiped the perspiration from his brow.

'That is no light part of my penance,' pursued the Ghost. 'I am here to-night to warn you, that you have yet a chance and hope of escaping my fate. A chance and hope of my procuring, Ebenezer.'

'You were always a good friend to me,' said Scrooge. 'Thank'ee!'

'You will be haunted,' resumed the Ghost, 'by Three Spirits.'

Scrooge's countenance fell almost as low as the Ghost's had done.

'Is that the chance and hope you mentioned, Jacob?' he demanded, in a faltering voice.

'It is.'

'I – I think I'd rather not,' said Scrooge.

'Without their visits,' said the Ghost, 'you cannot hope to shun the path I tread. Expect the first to-morrow, when the bell tolls one.'

'Couldn't I take 'em all at once, and have it over, Jacob?' hinted Scrooge.

'Expect the second on the next night at the same hour. The third upon the next night when the last stroke of twelve has ceased to vibrate. Look to see me no more; and look that, for your own sake, you remember what has passed between us!'

When it had said these words, the spectre took its wrapper from the table, and bound it round its head, as before. Scrooge knew this, by the smart sound its teeth made, when the jaws were brought together by the bandage. He ventured to raise his eyes again, and found his supernatural visitor confronting him in an erect attitude, with its chain wound over and about its arm.

The apparition walked backward from him; and at every step it took, the window raised itself a little, so that when the spectre reached it, it was wide open. It beckoned Scrooge to approach, which he did. When they were within two paces of each other, Marley's Ghost held up its hand, warning him to come no nearer. Scrooge stopped.

Not so much in obedience, as in surprise and fear: for on the raising of the hand, he became sensible of confused noises in the air; incoherent sounds of lamentation and regret; wailings inexpressibly sorrowful and self-accusatory. The spectre, after listening for a moment, joined in the mournful dirge; and floated out upon the bleak, dark night.

Scrooge followed to the window: desperate in his curiosity. He looked out.

The air was filled with phantoms, wandering hither and thither in restless haste, and moaning as they went. Every one of them wore chains like Marley's Ghost; some few (they might be guilty governments) were linked together; none were free. Many had been personally known to Scrooge in their lives. He had been quite familiar with one old ghost, in a white waistcoat, with a monstrous iron safe attached to its ankle, who cried piteously at being unable to assist a wretched woman with an infant, whom it saw below, upon a door-step. The misery with them all was, clearly, that they sought to interfere, for good, in human matters, and had lost the power for ever.

Whether these creatures faded into mist, or mist enshrouded them, he could not tell. But they and their spirit voices faded together; and the night became as it had been when he walked home.

Scrooge closed the window, and examined the door by which the Ghost had entered. It was double-locked, as he had locked it with his own hands, and the bolts were undisturbed. He tried to say 'Humbug!' but stopped at the first syllable. And being, from the emotion he had undergone, or the fatigues of the day, or his glimpse of the Invisible World, or the dull conversation of the Ghost, or the lateness of the hour, much in need of repose; went straight to bed, without undressing, and fell asleep upon the instant.

STAVE 2

The First of the Three Spirits

When Scrooge awoke, it was so dark, that looking out of bed, he could scarcely distinguish the transparent window from the opaque walls of his chamber. He was endeavouring to pierce the darkness with his ferret eyes, when the chimes of a neighbouring church struck the four quarters. So he listened for the hour.

To his great astonishment the heavy bell went on from six to seven, and from seven to eight, and regularly up to twelve; then stopped. Twelve! It was past two when he went to bed. The clock was wrong. An icicle must have got into the works. Twelve!

He touched the spring of his repeater, to correct this most preposterous clock. Its rapid little pulse beat twelve; and stopped.

'Why, it isn't possible,' said Scrooge, 'that I can have slept through a whole day and far into another night. It isn't possible that anything has happened to the sun, and this is twelve at noon.'

The idea being an alarming one, he scrambled out of bed, and groped his way to the window. He was obliged to rub the frost off with the sleeve of his dressing-gown before he could see anything; and could see very little then. All he could make out was, that it was still very foggy and extremely cold, and that there was no noise of people running to and fro, and making a great stir, as there unquestionably would have been if night had beaten off bright day, and taken possession of the world. This was a great relief, because "three days after sight of this First of Exchange pay to Mr. Ebenezer Scrooge or his order," and so forth, would have become a mere United States' security if there were no days to count by.

Scrooge went to bed again, and thought, and thought, and thought it over and over and over, and could make nothing of it. The more he thought, the more perplexed he was; and the more he endeavored not to think, the more he thought. Marley's Ghost bothered him exceedingly. Every time he resolved within himself, after mature inquiry, that it was all a dream, his mind flew back again, like a strong spring released, to its first position, and presented the same problem to be worked all through, "Was it a dream or not?"

Scrooge lay in this state until the chimes had gone three quarters more, when he remembered, on a sudden, that the Ghost had warned him of a visitation when the bell tolled one. He resolved to lie awake until the hour was past; and, considering that he could no more go to sleep than go to Heaven, this was perhaps the wisest resolution in his power.

The quarter was so long, that he was more than once convinced he must have sunk into a doze unconsciously, and missed the clock. At length it broke upon his listening ear.

'Ding, dong!'

'A quarter past,' said Scrooge, counting.

'Ding dong!'

'Half past!' said Scrooge.

'Ding dong!'

'A quarter to it,' said Scrooge.

'Ding dong!'

'The hour itself,' said Scrooge, triumphantly,

'and nothing else!'

He spoke before the hour bell sounded, which it now did with a deep, dull, hollow, melancholy One. Light flashed up in the room upon the instant, and the curtains of his bed were drawn.

The curtains of his bed were drawn aside, I tell you, by a hand. Not the curtains at his feet, nor the curtains at his back, but those to which his face was addressed. The curtains of his bed were drawn aside; and Scrooge, starting up into a half-recumbent attitude, found himself face to face with the unearthly visitor who drew them: as close to it as I am now to you, and I am standing in the spirit at your elbow.

It was a strange figure – like a child: yet not so like a child as like an old man, viewed through some supernatural medium, which gave him the appearance of having receded from the view, and being diminished to a child's proportions. Its hair, which hung about its neck and down its back, was white as if with age; and yet the face had not a wrinkle in it, and the tenderest bloom was on the skin. The arms were very long and muscular; the hands the same, as if its hold were of uncommon strength. Its legs and feet, most delicately formed, were, like those upper members, bare. It wore a tunic of the purest white; and round its waist was bound a lustrous belt, the sheen of which was beautiful. It held a branch of fresh green holly in its hand; and, in singular contradiction of that wintry emblem, had its dress trimmed with summer flowers. But the strangest thing about it was, that from the crown of its head there sprung a bright clear jet of light, by which all this was visible; and which was doubtless the occasion of its using, in its duller moments, a great extinguisher for a cap, which it now held under its arm.

Even this, though, when Scrooge looked at it with increasing steadiness, was *not* its strangest quality. For as its belt sparkled and glittered now in one part and now in another, and what was light one instant, at another time was dark, so the figure itself fluctuated in its distinctness: being now a thing with one arm, now with one leg, now with twenty legs, now a pair of legs without a head, now a head without a body: of which dissolving parts, no outline would be visible in the dense gloom wherein they melted away. And in the very wonder of this, it would be itself again; distinct and clear as ever.

'Are you the Spirit, sir, whose coming was foretold to me?' asked Scrooge.

'I am!'

The voice was soft and gentle. Singularly low, as if instead of being so close beside him, it were at a distance.

'Who, and what are you?' Scrooge demanded.

'I am the Ghost of Christmas Past.'

'Long past?' inquired Scrooge: observant of its dwarfish stature.

'No. Your past.'

Perhaps, Scrooge could not have told anybody why, if anybody could have asked him; but he had a special desire to see the Spirit in his cap; and begged him to be covered.

'What!' exclaimed the Ghost, 'would you so soon put out, with worldly hands, the light I give? Is it not enough that you are one of those whose passions made this cap, and force me through whole trains of years to wear it low upon my brow!'

Scrooge reverently disclaimed all intention to offend, or any knowledge of having wilfully 'bonneted' the Spirit at any period of his life. He then made bold to inquire what business brought him there.

'Your welfare!' said the Ghost.

Scrooge expressed himself much obliged, but could not help thinking that a night of unbroken rest would have been more conducive to that end. The Spirit must have heard him thinking, for it said immediately:

'Your reclamation, then. Take heed!'

It put out its strong hand as it spoke, and clasped him gently by the arm.

'Rise! and walk with me!'

It would have been in vain for Scrooge to plead that the weather and the hour were not adapted to pedestrian purposes; that bed was warm, and the thermometer a long way below freezing; that he was clad but lightly in his slippers, dressing-gown, and nightcap; and that he had a cold upon him at that time. The grasp, though gentle as a woman's hand, was not to be resisted. He rose: but finding that the Spirit made towards the window, clasped his robe in supplication.

'I am mortal,' Scrooge remonstrated, 'and liable to fall.'

'Bear but a touch of my hand *there*,' said the Spirit, laying it upon his heart, 'and you shall be upheld in more than this!'

As the words were spoken, they passed through the wall, and stood upon an open country road, with fields on either hand. The city had entirely vanished. Not a vestige of it was to be seen. The darkness and the mist had vanished with it, for it was a clear, cold, winter day, with snow upon the ground.

'Good Heaven!' said Scrooge, clasping his hands together, as he looked about him. 'I was bred in this place. I was a boy here!'

The Spirit gazed upon him mildly. Its gentle touch, though it had been light and instantaneous, appeared still present to the old man's sense of feeling. He was conscious of a thousand odours floating in the air, each one connected with a thousand thoughts, and hopes, and joys, and cares long, long, forgotten!

'Your lip is trembling,' said the Ghost. 'And what is that upon your cheek.'

Scrooge muttered, with an unusual catching in his voice, that it was a pimple; and begged the Ghost to lead him where he would.

'You recollect the way?' inquired the Spirit.

'Remember it!' cried Scrooge with fervour – 'I could walk it blindfold.'

'Strange to have forgotten it for so many years!' observed the Ghost. 'Let us go on.'

They walked along the road, Scrooge recognising every gate, and post, and tree; until a little market-town appeared in the distance, with its bridge, its church, and winding river. Some shaggy ponies now were seen trotting towards them with boys upon their backs, who called to other boys in country gigs and carts, driven by farmers. All these boys were in great spirits, and shouted to each other, until the broad fields were so full of merry music, that the crisp air laughed to hear it.

'These are but shadows of the things that have been,' said the Ghost. 'They have no consciousness of us.'

The jocund travellers came on; and as they came, Scrooge knew and named them every one. Why was he rejoiced beyond all bounds to see them! Why did his cold eye glisten, and his heart leap up as they went past! Why was he filled with gladness when he heard them give each other Merry Christmas, as they parted at cross-roads and bye-ways, for their several homes! What was merry Christmas to Scrooge? Out upon merry Christmas! What good had it ever done to him?

'The school is not quite deserted,' said the Ghost. 'A solitary child, neglected by his friends, is left there still.'

Scrooge said he knew it. And he sobbed.

They left the high-road, by a well remembered lane, and soon approached a mansion of dull red brick, with a little weathercock-surmounted cupola, on the roof, and a bell hanging in it. It was a large house, but one of broken fortunes; for the spacious offices were little used, their walls were damp and mossy, their windows broken, and their gates decayed. Fowls clucked and strutted in the stables; and the coach-houses and sheds were over-run with grass. Nor was it more retentive of its ancient state, within; for entering the dreary hall, and glancing through the open doors of many rooms, they found them poorly furnished, cold, and vast. There was an earthy savour in the air, a chilly bareness in the place, which associated itself somehow with too much getting up by candle-light, and not too much to eat.

They went, the Ghost and Scrooge, across the hall, to a door at the back of the house. It opened before them, and disclosed a long, bare, melancholy room, made barer still by lines of plain deal forms and desks. At one of these a lonely boy was reading near a feeble fire; and Scrooge sat down upon a form, and wept to see his poor forgotten self as he used to be.

Not a latent echo in the house, not a squeak and scuffle from the mice behind the panelling, not a drip from the half-thawed water-spout in the dull yard behind, not a sigh among the leafless boughs of one despondent poplar, not the idle swinging of an empty store-house door, no, not a clicking in the fire, but fell upon the heart of Scrooge with a softening influence, and gave a freer passage to his tears.

The Spirit touched him on the arm, and pointed to his younger self, intent upon his reading. Suddenly a man, in foreign garments: wonderfully real and distinct to look at: stood outside the window, with an axe stuck in his belt, and leading an ass laden with wood by the bridle.

'Why, it's Ali Baba!' Scrooge exclaimed in ecstasy. 'It's dear old honest Ali Baba! Yes, yes, I know!. One Christmas time, when yonder solitary child was left here all alone, he *did* come, for the first time, just like that. Poor boy! And Valentine,' said Scrooge, 'and his wild brother, Orson; there they go! And what's his name, who was put down in his drawers, asleep, at the Gate of Damascus; don't you see him! And the Sultan's Groom turned upside-down by the Genii; there he is upon his head! Serve him right. I'm glad of it. What business had *he* to be married to the Princess!'

To hear Scrooge expending all the earnestness of his nature on such subjects, in a most extraordinary voice between laughing and crying; and to see his heightened and excited face; would have been a surprise to his business friends in the city, indeed.

'There's the Parrot!' cried Scrooge. 'Green body and yellow tail, with a thing like a lettuce growing out of the top of his head; there he is! Poor Robin Crusoe, he called him, when he came home again after sailing round the island. "Poor Robin Crusoe, where have you been, Robin Crusoe?" The man thought he was dreaming, but he wasn't. It was the Parrot, you know. There goes Friday, running for his life to the little creek! Halloa! Hoop! Halloo!'

Then, with a rapidity of transition very foreign to his usual character, he said, in pity for his former self, 'Poor boy!' and cried again.

'I wish,' Scrooge muttered, putting his hand in his pocket, and looking about him, after drying his eyes with his cuff: 'but it's too late now.'

'What is the matter?' asked the Spirit.

'Nothing,' said Scrooge. 'Nothing. There was a boy singing a Christmas Carol at my door last night. I should like to have given him something: that's all.'

The Ghost smiled thoughtfully, and waved its hand: saying as it did so, 'Let us see another Christmas!'

Scrooge's former self grew larger at the words, and the room became a little darker and more dirty. The panels shrunk, the windows cracked; fragments of plaster fell out of the ceiling, and the naked laths were shown instead; but how all this was brought about, Scrooge knew no more than you do. He only knew that it was quite correct; that everything had happened so; that there he was, alone again, when all the other boys had gone home for the jolly holidays.

He was not reading now, but walking up and down despairingly. Scrooge looked at the Ghost, and with a mournful shaking of his head, glanced anxiously towards the door.

It opened; and a little girl, much younger than the boy, came darting in, and putting her arms about his neck, and often kissing him, addressed him as her 'Dear, dear brother.'

'I have come to bring you home, dear brother!' said the child, clapping her tiny hands, and bending down to laugh. 'To bring you home, home, home!'

'Home, little Fan?' returned the boy.

'Yes!' said the child, brimful of glee. 'Home, for good and all. Home, for ever and ever. Father is so much kinder than he used to be, that home's like Heaven! He spoke so gently to me one dear night when I was going to bed, that I was not afraid to ask him once more if you might come home; and he said Yes, you should; and sent me in a coach to bring you. And you're to be a man!' said the child, opening her eyes, 'and are never to come back here; but first, we're to be together all the Christmas long, and have the merriest time in all the world.'

'You are quite a woman, little Fan!' exclaimed the boy.

She clapped her hands and laughed, and tried to touch his head; but being too little, laughed again, and stood on tiptoe to embrace him. Then she began to drag him, in her childish eagerness, towards the door; and he, nothing loth to go, accompanied her.

A terrible voice in the hall cried. 'Bring down Master Scrooge's box, there!' and in the hall appeared the schoolmaster himself, who glared on Master Scrooge with a ferocious condescension, and threw him into a dreadful state of mind by shaking hands with him. He then conveyed him and his sister into the veriest old well of a shivering best-parlour that ever was seen, where the maps upon the wall, and the celestial and terrestrial globes in the windows, were waxy with cold. Here he produced a decanter of curiously light wine, and a block of curiously heavy cake, and administered instalments of those dainties to the young people: at the same time, sending out a meagre servant to offer a glass of 'something' to the postboy, who answered that he thanked the gentleman, but if it was the same tap as he had tasted before, he had rather not. Master Scrooge's trunk being by this time tied on to the top of the chaise, the children bade the schoolmaster good-bye right willingly; and getting into it, drove gaily down the garden-sweep: the quick wheels dashing the hoar-frost and snow from off the dark leaves of the evergreens like spray.

'Always a delicate creature, whom a breath might have withered,' said the Ghost. 'But she had a large heart.'

'So she had,' cried Scrooge. 'You're right. I will not gainsay it, Spirit. God forbid!'

'She died a woman,' said the Ghost, 'and had, as I think, children.'

'One child,' Scrooge returned.

'True,' said the Ghost. 'Your nephew!'

Scrooge seemed uneasy in his mind; and answered briefly, 'Yes.'

Although they had but that moment left the school behind them, they were now in the busy thoroughfares of a city, where shadowy passengers passed and repassed; where shadowy carts and coaches battle for the way, and all the strife and tumult of a real city were. It was made plain enough, by the dressing of the shops, that here too it was Christmas time again; but it was evening, and the streets were lighted up.

The Ghost stopped at a certain warehouse door, and asked Scrooge if he knew it.

'Know it!' said Scrooge. 'Was I apprenticed here?'

They went in. At sight of an old gentleman in a Welch wig, sitting behind such a high desk, that if he had been two inches taller he must have knocked his head against the ceiling, Scrooge cried in great excitement:

'Why, it's old Fezziwig! Bless his heart; it's Fezziwig alive again!'

Old Fezziwig laid down his pen, and looked up at the clock, which pointed to the hour of seven. He rubbed his hands; adjusted his capacious waistcoat; laughed all over himself, from his shows to his organ of benevolence; and called out in a comfortable, oily, rich, fat, jovial voice:

'Yo ho, there! Ebenezer! Dick!'

Scrooge's former self, now grown a young man, came briskly in, accompanied by his fellow-'prentice.

'Dick Wilkins, to be sure!' said Scrooge to the Ghost. 'Bless me, yes. There he is. He was very much attached to me, was Dick. Poor Dick! Dear, dear!'

'Yo ho, my boys!' said Fezziwig. 'No more work to-night. Christmas Eve, Dick. Christmas, Ebenezer! Let's have the shutters up,' cried old Fezziwig, with a sharp clap of his hands, 'before a man can say Jack Robinson.'

You wouldn't believe how those two fellows went at it! They charged into the street with the shutters – one, two, three – had them up in their places – four, five, six – barred 'em and pinned 'em – seven, eight, nine – and came back before you could have got to twelve, panting like race-horses.

'Hilli-ho!' cried old Fezziwig, skipping down from the high desk, with wonderful agility. 'Clear away, my lads, and let's have lots of room here! Hilli-ho, Dick! Chirrup, Ebenezer!'

Clear away! There was nothing they wouldn't have cleared away, or couldn't have cleared away, with old Fezziwig looking on. It was done in a minute. Every movable was packed off, as if it were dismissed from public life for evermore; the floor was swept and watered, the lamps were trimmed, fuel was heaped upon the fire; and the warehouse was as snug, and warm, and dry, and bright a ball-room, as you would desire to see upon a winter's night.

In came a fiddler with a music-book, and went up to the lofty desk, and made an orchestra of it, and tuned like fifty stomach-aches. In came Mrs. Fezziwig, one vast substantial smile. In came the three Miss Fezziwigs, beaming and lovable. In came the six young followers whose hearts they broke. In came all the young men and women employed in the business. In came the housemaid, with her cousin, the baker. In came the cook, with her brother's particular friend, the milkman. In came the boy from over the way, who was suspected of not having board enough from his master; trying to hide himself behind the girl from next door but one, who was proved to have had her ears pulled by her mistress. In they all came, one after another; some shyly, some boldly, some gracefully, some awkwardly, some pushing, some pulling; in they all came, anyhow and everyhow. Away they all went, twenty couple at once; hands half round and back again the other way; down the middle and up again; round and round in various stages of affectionate grouping; old top couple always turning up in the wrong place; new top couple starting off again, as soon as they got there; all top couples at last, and not a bottom one to help them. When this result was brought about, old Fezziwig, clapping his hands to stop the dance, cried out, 'Well done!' and the fiddler plunged his hot face into a pot of porter, especially provided for that purpose. But scorning rest upon his reappearance, he instantly began again, though there were no dancers yet, as if the other fiddler had been carried home, exhausted, on a shutter; and he were a bran-new man resolved to beat him out of sight, or perish.

There were more dances, and there were forfeits, and more dances, and there was cake, and there was negus, and there was a great piece of Cold Roast, and there was a great piece of Cold Boiled, and there were mince-pies, and plenty of beer. But the great effect of the evening came after the Roast and Boiled, when the fiddler (an artful dog, mind! The sort of man who knew his business better than you or I could have told it him!) struck up 'Sir Roger de Coverley'. Then old Fezziwig stood out to dance with Mrs. Fezziwig. Top couple, too; with a good stiff piece of work cut out for them; three or four and twenty pair of partners; people who were not to be trifled with; people who *would* dance, and had no notion of walking.

But if they had been twice as many: ah, four times: old Fezziwig would have been a match for them, and so would Mrs. Fezziwig. As to *her*, she was worthy to be his partner in every sense of the term. If that's not high praise, tell me higher, and I'll use it. A positive light appeared to issue from Fezziwig's calves. They shone in every part of the dance like moons. You couldn't have predicted, at any given time, what would have become of 'em next. And when old Fezziwig and Mrs. Fezziwig had gone all through the dance; advance and retire, hold hands with your partner; bow and curtsey; corkscrew; thread-the needle, and back again to your place; Fezziwig 'cut' – cut so deftly, that he appeared to wink with his legs, and came upon his feet again without a stagger.

When the clock struck eleven, this domestic ball broke up. Mr. and Mrs. Fezziwig took their stations, one on either side the door, and shaking hands with every person individually as he or she went out, wished him or her a Merry Christmas. When everybody had retired but the two 'prentices, they did the same to them; and thus the cheerful voices died away, and the lads were left to their beds; which were under a counter in the back-shop.

During the whole of this time, Scrooge had acted like a man out of his wits. His heart and soul were in the scene, and with his former self. He corroborated everything, remembered everything, enjoyed everything, and underwent the strangest agitation. It was not until now, when the bright faces of his former self and Dick were turned from them, that he remembered the Ghost, and became conscious that it was looking full upon him, while the light upon its head burnt very clear.

'A small matter,' said the Ghost, 'to make these silly folks so full of gratitude.'

'Small!' echoed Scrooge.

The Spirit signed to him to listen to the two apprentices, who were pouring out their hearts in praise of Fezziwig: and when he had done so, said, 'Why! Is it not? He has spent but a few pounds of your mortal money: three or four perhaps. Is that so much that he deserves this praise?'

'It isn't that,' said Scrooge, heated by the remark, and speaking unconsciously like his former, not his latter, self. 'It isn't that, Spirit. He has the power to render us happy or unhappy; to make our service light or burdensome; a pleasure or a toil. Say that his power lies in words and looks; in things so slight and insignificant that it is impossible to add and count 'em up: what then? The happiness he gives, is quite as great as if it cost a fortune.'

He felt the Spirit's glance, and stopped.

'What is the matter?' asked the Ghost.

'Nothing particular,' said Scrooge.

'Something, I think?' the Ghost insisted.

'No,' said Scrooge, 'No. I should like to be able to say a word or two to my clerk just now! That's all.'

His former self turned down the lamps as he gave utterance to the wish; and Scrooge and the Ghost again stood side by side in the open air.

'My time grows short,' observed the Spirit. 'Quick!'

This was not addressed to Scrooge, or to any one whom he could see, but it produced an immediate effect. For again Scrooge saw himself. He was older now; a man in the prime of life. His face had not the harsh and rigid lines of later years; but it had begun to wear the signs of care and avarice. There was an eager, greedy, restless motion in the eye, which showed the passion that had taken root, and where the shadow of the growing tree would fall.

He was not alone, but sat by the side of a fair young girl in a mourning-dress: in whose eyes there were tears, which sparkled in the light that shone out of the Ghost of Christmas Past.

'It matters little,' she said, softly. 'To you, very little. Another idol has displaced me; and if it can cheer and comfort you in time to come, as I would have tried to do, I have no just cause to grieve.'

'What Idol has displaced you?' he rejoined.

'A golden one.'

'This is the even-handed dealing of the world!' he said. 'There is nothing on which it is so hard as poverty; and there is nothing it professes to condemn with such severity as the pursuit of wealth!'

'You fear the world too much,' she answered, gently. 'All your other hopes have merged into the hope of being beyond the chance of its sordid reproach. I have seen your nobler aspirations fall off one by one, until the master-passion, Gain, engrosses you. Have I not?'

'What then?' he retorted. 'Even if I have grown so much wiser, what then? I am not changed towards you.'

She shook her head.

'Am I?'

'Our contract is an old one. It was made when we were both poor and content to be so, until, in good season, we could improve our worldly fortune by our patient industry. You *are* changed. When it was made, you were another man.'

'I was a boy,' he said impatiently.

'Your own feeling tells you that you were not what you are,' she returned. 'I am. That which promised happiness when we were one in heart, is fraught with misery now that we are two. How often and how keenly I have thought of this, I will not say. It is enough that I *have* thought of it, and can release you.'

'Have I ever sought release?'

'In words. No. Never.'

'In what, then?'

'In a changed nature; in an altered spirit; in another atmosphere of life; another Hope as its great end. In everything that made my love of any worth or value in your sight. If this had never been between us,' said the girl, looking mildly, but with steadiness, upon him; 'tell me, would you seek me out and try to win me now? Ah, no!'

He seemed to yield to the justice of this supposition, in spite of himself. But he said, with a struggle, 'You think not.'

'I would gladly think otherwise if I could,' she answered, 'Heaven knows. When *I* have learned a Truth like this, I know how strong and irresistible it must be. But if you were free to-day, to-morrow, yesterday, can even I believe that you would choose a dowerless girl – you who, in your very confidence with her, weigh everything by Gain: or, choosing her, if for a moment you were false enough to your one guiding principle to do so, do I not know that your repentance and regret would surely follow? I do; and I release you. With a full heart, for the love of him you once were.'

He was about to speak; but with her head turned from him, she resumed.

'You may – the memory of what is past half makes me hope you will – have pain in this. A very, very brief time, and you will dismiss the recollection of it, gladly, as an unprofitable dream, from which it happened well that you awoke. May you be happy in the life you have chosen!'

She left him; and they parted.

'Spirit!' said Scrooge, 'show me no more! Conduct me home. Why do you delight to torture me?'

'One shadow more!' exclaimed the Ghost.

'No more!' cried Scrooge. 'No more. I don't wish to see it. Show me no more!'

But the relentless Ghost pinioned him in both his arms, and forced him to observe what happened next.

They were in another scene and place: a room, not very large or handsome, but full of comfort. Near to the winter fire sat a beautiful young girl, so like that last that Scrooge believed it was the same, until he saw *her*, now a comely matron, sitting opposite her daughter. The noise in this room was perfectly tumultuous, for there were more children there, than Scrooge in his agitated state of mind could count; and, unlike the celebrated herd in the poem, they were not forty children conducting themselves like one, but every child was conducting itself like forty. The consequences were uproarious beyond belief; but no one seemed to care; on the contrary, the mother and daughter laughed heartily, and enjoyed it very much; and the latter, soon beginning to mingle in the sports, got pillaged by the young brigands most ruthlessly. What would I not have given to be one of them! Though I never could have been so rude, no, no! I wouldn't for the wealth of all the world have crushed that braided hair, and torn it down; and for the precious little shoe, I wouldn't have plucked it off, God bless my soul! to save my life. As to measuring her waist in sport, as they did, bold young brood, I couldn't have done it; I should have expected my arm to have grown round it for a punishment, and never come straight again. And yet I should have dearly liked, I own, to have touched her lips; to have questioned her, that she might have opened them; to have looked upon the lashes of her downcast eyes, and never raised a blush; to have let loose waves of hair, an inch of which would be a keepsake beyond price: in short, I should have liked, I do confess, to have had the lightest licence of a child, and yet to have been man enough to know its value.

But now a knocking at the door was heard, and such a rush immediately ensued that she with laughing face and plundered dress was borne towards it the centre of a flushed and boisterous group, just in time to greet the father, who came home attended by a man laden with Christmas toys and presents. Then the shouting and the struggling, and the onslaught that was made on the defenceless porter! The scaling him with chairs for ladders to dive into his pockets, despoil him of brown-paper parcels, hold on tight by his cravat, hug him round his neck, pommel his back, and kick his legs in irrepressible affection! The shouts of wonder and delight with which the development of every package was received! The terrible announcement that the baby had been taken in the act of putting a doll's frying-pan into his mouth, and was more than suspected of having swallowed a fictitious turkey, glued on a wooden platter! The immense relief of finding this a false alarm. The joy, and gratitude, and ecstasy! They are all indescribable alike. It is enough that by degrees the children and their emotions got out of the parlour and by one stair at a time, up to the top of the house; where they went to bed, and so subsided.

And now Scrooge looked on more attentively than ever, when the master of the house, having his daughter leaning fondly on him, sat down with her and her mother at his own fireside; and when he thought that such another creature, quite as graceful and as full of promise, might have called him father, and been a spring-time in the haggard winter of his life, his sight grew very dim indeed.

'Belle,' said the husband, turning to his wife with a smile, 'I saw an old friend of yours this afternoon.'

'Who was it?'

'Guess!'

'How can I? Tut, don't I know,' she added in the same breath, laughing as he laughed. 'Mr Scrooge.'

'Mr Scrooge it was. I passed his office window; and as it was not shut up, and he had a candle inside, I could scarcely help seeing him. His partner lies upon the point of death, I hear; and there he sat alone. Quite alone in the world, I do believe.'

'Spirit!' said Scrooge in a broken voice, 'remove me from this place.'

'I told you these were shadows of the things that have been,' said the Ghost. 'That they are what they are, do not blame me!'

'Remove me!' Scrooge exclaimed, 'I cannot bear it!'

He turned upon the Ghost, and seeing that it looked upon him with a face, in which in some strange way there were fragments of all the faces it had shown him, wrestled with it.

'Leave me! Take me back. Haunt me no longer!'

In the struggle, if that can be called a struggle in which the Ghost with no visible resistance on its own part was undisturbed by any effort of its adversary, Scrooge observed that its light was burning high and bright; and dimly connecting that with its influence over him, he seized the extinguisher-cap, and by a sudden action pressed it down upon its head.

The Spirit dropped beneath it, so that the extinguisher covered its whole form; but though Scrooge pressed it down with all his force, he could not hide the light: which streamed from under it, in an unbroken flood upon the ground.

He was conscious of being exhausted, and overcome by an irresistible drowsiness; and, further, of being in his own bedroom. He gave the cap a parting squeeze, in which his hand relaxed; and had barely time to reel to bed, before he sank into a heavy sleep.

The Second of the Three Spirits

Awaking in the middle of a prodigiously tough snore, and sitting up in bed to get his thoughts together, Scrooge had no occasion to be told that the bell was again upon the stroke of One. He felt that he was restored to consciousness in the right nick of time, for the especial purpose of holding a conference with the second messenger despatched to him through Jacob Marley's intervention. But finding that he turned uncomfortably cold when he began to wonder which of his curtains this new spectre would draw back, he put them every one aside with his own hands; and lying down again, established a sharp look-out all round the bed. For he wished to challenge the Spirit on the moment of its appearance, and did not wish to be taken by surprise and made nervous.

Gentlemen of the free-and-easy sort, who plume themselves on being acquainted with a move or two, and being usually equal to the time-of-day, express the wide range of their capacity for adventure by observing that they are good for anything from pitch-and-toss to manslaughter; between which opposite extremes, no doubt, there lies a tolerably wide and comprehensive range of subjects. Without venturing for Scrooge quite as hardily as this, I don't mind calling on you to believe that he was ready for a good broad field of strange appearances, and that nothing between a baby and a rhinoceros would have astonished him very much.

Now, being prepared for almost anything, he was not by any means prepared for nothing; and, consequently, when the Bell struck One, and no shape appeared, he was taken with a violent fit of trembling. Five minutes, ten minutes, a quarter of an hour went by, yet nothing came. All this time, he lay upon his bed, the very core and centre of a blaze of ruddy light, which streamed upon it when the clock proclaimed the hour; and which being only light, was more alarming than a dozen ghosts, as he was powerless to make out what it meant, or would be at; and was sometimes apprehensive that he might be at that very moment an interesting case of spontaneous combustion, without having the consolation of knowing it. At last, however, he began to think – as you or I would have thought at first; for it is always the person not in the predicament who knows what ought to have been done in it, and would unquestionably have done it too – at last, I say, he began to think that the source and secret of this ghostly light might be in the adjoining room: from whence, on further tracing it, it seemed to shine. This idea taking full possession of his mind, he got up softly and shuffled in his slippers to the door.

The moment Scrooge's hand was on the lock, a strange voice called him by his name, and bade him enter. He obeyed.

It was his own room. There was no doubt about that. But it had undergone a surprising transformation. The walls and ceiling were so hung with living green, that it looked a perfect grove; from every part of which, bright gleaming berries glistened. The crisp leaves of holly, mistletoe, and ivy reflected back the light, as if so many little mirrors had been scattered there; and such a mighty blaze went roaring up the chimney, as that dull petrification of a hearth had never known in Scrooge's time, or Marley's, or for many and many a winter season gone. Heaped upon the floor, to form a kind of throne, were turkeys, geese, game, poultry, brawn, great joints of meat, sucking-pigs, long wreaths of sausages, mince-pies, plum-puddings, barrels of oysters, red-hot chestnuts, cherry-cheeked apples, juicy oranges, luscious pears, immense twelfth-cakes, and seething bowls of punch, that made the chamber dim with their delicious steam. In easy state upon this couch, there sat a jolly Giant, glorious to see; who bore a glowing torch, in shape not unlike Plenty's horn, and held it up, high up, to shed its light on Scrooge, as he came peeping round the door.

'Come in!' exclaimed the Ghost. 'Come in! and know me better, man!'

Scrooge entered timidly, and hung his head before this Spirit. He was not the dogged Scrooge he had been; and though its eyes were clear and kind, he did not like to meet them.

'I am the Ghost of Christmas Present,' said the Spirit. 'Look upon me!'

Scrooge reverently did so. It was clothed in one simple deep green robe, or mantle, bordered with white fur. This garment hung so loosely on the figure, that its capacious breast was bare, as if disdaining to be warded or concealed by any artifice. Its feet, observable beneath the ample folds of the garment, were also bare; and on its head it wore no other covering than a holly wreath, set here and there with shining icicles. Its dark brown curls were long and free: free as its genial face, its sparkling eye, its open hand, its cheery voice, its unconstrained demeanour, and its joyful air. Girded round its middle was an antique scabbard; but no sword was in it, and the ancient sheath was eaten up with rust.

'You have never seen the like of me before!' exclaimed the Spirit.

'Never,' Scrooge made answer to it.

'Have never walked forth with the younger members of my family; meaning (for I am very young) my elder brothers born in these later years?' pursued the Phantom.

'I don't think I have,' said Scrooge. 'I am afraid I have not. Have you had many brothers, Spirit?'

'More than eighteen hundred,' said the Ghost.

'A tremendous family to provide for!' muttered Scrooge.

The Ghost of Christmas Present rose.

'Spirit,' said Scrooge submissively, 'conduct me where you will. I went forth last night on compulsion, and I learnt a lesson which is working now. To-night, if you have aught to teach me, let me profit by it.'

'Touch my robe!'

Scrooge did as he was told, and held it fast.

Holly, mistletoe, red berries, ivy, turkeys, geese, game, poultry, brawn, meat, pigs, sausages, oysters, pies, puddings, fruit, and punch, all vanished instantly. So did the room, the fire, the ruddy glow, the hour of night, and they stood in the city streets on Christmas morning, where (for the weather was severe) the people made a rough, but brisk and not unpleasant kind of music, in scraping the snow from the pavement in front of their dwellings, and from the tops of their houses, whence it was mad delight to the boys to see it come plumping down into the road below, and splitting into artificial little snowstorms.

The house fronts looked black enough, and the windows blacker, contrasting with the smooth white sheet of snow upon the roofs, and with the dirtier snow upon the ground; which last deposit had been ploughed up in deep furrows by the heavy wheels of carts and waggons; furrows that crossed and re-crossed each other hundreds of times where the great streets branched off, and made intricate channels, hard to trace in the thick yellow mud and icy water. The sky was gloomy, and the shortest streets were choked up with a dingy mist, half thawed, half frozen, whose heavier particles descended in a shower of sooty atoms, as if all the chimneys in Great Britain had, by one consent, caught fire, and were blazing away to their dear hearts' content. There was nothing very cheerful in the climate or the town, and yet was there an air of cheerfulness abroad that the clearest summer air and brightest summer sun might have endeavoured to diffuse in vain.

For the people who were shovelling away on the housetops were jovial and full of glee; calling out to one another from the parapets, and now and then exchanging a facetious snowball – better-natured missile far than many a wordy jest – laughing heartily if it went right and not less heartily if it went wrong. The poulterers' shops were still half open, and the fruiterers' were radiant in their glory. There were great, round, pot-bellied baskets of chestnuts, shaped like the waistcoats of jolly old gentlemen, lolling at the doors, and tumbling out into the street in their apoplectic opulence. There were ruddy, brown-faced, broad-girthed Spanish Onions, shining in the fatness of their growth like Spanish Friars; and winking from their shelves in wanton slyness at the girls as they went by, and glanced demurely at the hung-up mistletoe. There were pears and apples, clustered high in blooming pyramids; there were bunches of grapes, made in the shopkeepers' benevolence to dangle from conspicuous hooks, that people's mouths might water gratis as they passed; there were piles of filberts, mossy and brown, recalling, in their fragrance, ancient walks among the woods, and pleasant shufflings ankle deep through withered leaves; there were Norfolk Biffins, squab and swarthy, setting off the yellow of the oranges and lemons, and, in the great compactness of their juicy persons, urgently entreating and beseeching to be carried home in paper bags and eaten after dinner. The very gold and silver fish, set forth among these choice fruits in a bowl, though members of a dull and stagnant-blooded race, appeared to know that there was something going on; and, to a fish, went gasping round and round their little world in slow and passionless excitement.

The Grocers'! oh the Grocers'! nearly closed, with perhaps two shutters down, or one; but through those gaps such glimpses! It was not alone that the scales descending on the counter made a merry sound, or that the twine and roller parted company so briskly, or that the canisters were rattled up and down like juggling tricks, or even that the blended scents of tea and coffee were so grateful to the nose, or even that the raisins were so plentiful and rare, the almonds so extremely white, the sticks of cinnamon so long and straight, the other spices so delicious, the candied fruits so caked and spotted with molten sugar as to make the coldest lookers-on feel faint and subsequently bilious. Nor was it that the figs were moist and pulpy, or that the French plums blushed in modest tartness from their highly-decorated boxes, or that everything was good to eat and in its Christmas dress: but the customers were all so hurried and so eager in the hopeful promise of the day, that they tumbled up against each other at the door, clashing their wicker baskets wildly, and left their purchases upon the counter, and came running back to fetch them, and committed hundreds of the like mistakes, in the best humour possible; while the Grocer and his people were so frank and fresh that the polished hearts with which they fastened their aprons behind might have been their own, worn outside for general inspection, and for Christmas daws to peck at if they chose.

But soon the steeples called good people all, to church and chapel, and away they came, flocking through the streets in their best clothes, and with their gayest faces. And at the same time there emerged from scores of bye streets, lanes, and nameless turnings, innumerable people, carrying their dinners to the bakers' shops. The sight of these poor revellers appeared to interest the Spirit very much, for he stood with Scrooge beside him in a baker's doorway, and taking off the covers as their bearers passed, sprinkled incense on their dinners from his torch. And it was a very uncommon kind of torch, for once or twice when there were angry words between some dinner-carriers who had jostled each other, he shed a few drops of water on them from it, and their good humour was restored directly. For they said, it was a shame to quarrel upon Christmas Day. And so it was! God love it, so it was!

In time the bells ceased, and the bakers' were shut up; and yet there was a genial shadowing forth of all these dinners and the progress of their cooking, in the thawed blotch of wet above each baker's oven; where the pavement smoked as if its stones were cooking too.

'Is there a peculiar flavour in what you sprinkle from your torch?' asked Scrooge.

'There is. My own.'

'Would it apply to any kind of dinner on this day?' asked Scrooge.

'To any kindly given. To a poor one most.'

'Why to a poor one most?' asked Scrooge.

'Because it needs it most.'

'Spirit,' said Scrooge, after a moment's thought, 'I wonder you, of all the beings in the many worlds about us, should desire to cramp these people's opportunities of innocent enjoyment.'

'I!' cried the Spirit.

'You would deprive them of their means of dining every seventh day, often the only day on which they can be said to dine at all,' said Scrooge. 'Wouldn't you?'

'I!' cried the Spirit.

'You seek to close these places on the Seventh Day,' said Scrooge. 'And it comes to the same thing.'

'*I* seek!' exclaimed the Spirit.

'Forgive me if I am wrong. It has been done in your name, or at least in that of your family,' said Scrooge.

'There are some upon this earth of yours,' returned the Spirit, 'who lay claim to know us, and who do their deeds of passion, pride, ill-will, hatred, envy, bigotry, and selfishness in our name who are as strange to us and all our kith and kin, as if they had never lived. Remember that, and charge their doings on themselves, not us.'

Scrooge promised that he would; and they went on, invisible, as they had been before, into the suburbs of the town. It was a remarkable quality of the Ghost (which Scrooge had observed at the baker's) that notwithstanding his gigantic size, he could accommodate himself to any place with ease; and that he stood beneath a low roof quite as gracefully and like a supernatural creature, as it was possible he could have done in any lofty hall.

And perhaps it was the pleasure the good Spirit had in showing off this power of his, or else it was his own kind, generous, hearty nature, and his sympathy with all poor men, that led him straight to Scrooge's clerk's; for there he went, and took Scrooge with him, holding to his robe; and on the threshold of the door the Spirit smiled, and stopped to bless Bob Cratchit's dwelling with the sprinkling of his torch. Think of that! Bob had but fifteen 'Bob' a-week himself; he pocketed on Saturdays but fifteen copies of his Christian name; and yet the Ghost of Christmas Present blessed his four-roomed house!

Then up rose Mrs. Cratchit, Cratchit's wife, dressed out but poorly in a twice-turned gown, but brave in ribbons, which are cheap and make a goodly show for sixpence; and she laid the cloth, assisted by Belinda Cratchit, second of her daughters, also brave in ribbons; while Master Peter Cratchit plunged a fork into the saucepan of potatoes, and getting the corners of his monstrous shirt collar (Bob's private property, conferred upon his son and heir in honour of the day) into his mouth, rejoiced to find himself so gallantly attired, and yearned to show his linen in the fashionable Parks. And now two smaller Cratchits, boy and girl, came tearing in, screaming that outside the baker's they had smelt the goose, and known it for their own; and basking in luxurious thoughts of sage-and-onion, these young Cratchits danced about the table, and exalted

Master Peter Cratchit to the skies, while he (not proud, although his collars nearly choked him) blew the fire, until the slow potatoes bubbling up, knocked loudly at the saucepan-lid to be let out and peeled.

'What has ever got your precious father then,' said Mrs Cratchit. 'And your brother, Tiny Tim; and Martha warn't as late last Christmas Day by half-an-hour!'

'Here's Martha, mother!' said a girl, appearing as she spoke.

'Here's Martha, mother!' cried the two young Cratchits. 'Hurrah. There's *such* a goose, Martha!'

'Why, bless your heart alive, my dear, how late you are!' said Mrs. Cratchit, kissing her a dozen times, and taking off her shawl and bonnet for her, with officious zeal.

'We'd a deal of work to finish up last night,' replied the girl, 'and had to clear away this morning, mother!'

'Well! Never mind so long as you are come,' said Mrs. Cratchit. 'Sit ye down before the fire, my dear, and have a warm, Lord bless ye!'

'No no! There's father coming,' cried the two young Cratchits, who were everywhere at once. 'Hide, Martha, hide!'

So Martha hid herself, and in came little Bob, the father, with at least three feet of comforter exclusive of the fringe, hanging down before him; and his thread-bare clothes darned up and brushed, to look seasonable; and Tiny Tim upon his shoulder. Alas for Tiny Tim, he bore a little crutch, and had his limbs supported by an iron frame!

'Why, where's our Martha?' cried Bob Cratchit, looking round.

'Not coming,' said Mrs. Cratchit.

'Not coming!' said Bob, with a sudden declension in his high spirits; for he had been Tim's blood horse all the way from church, and had come home rampant. 'Not coming upon Christmas Day!'

Martha didn't like to see him disappointed, if it were only in joke; so she came out prematurely from behind the closet door, and ran into his arms, while the two young Cratchits hustled Tiny Tim, and bore him off into the wash house, that he might hear the pudding singing in the copper.

'And how did little Tim behave?' asked Mrs. Cratchit, when she had rallied Bob on his credulity and Bob had hugged his daughter to his heart's content.

'As good as gold,' said Bob, 'and better. Somehow he gets thoughtful sitting by himself so much, and thinks the strangest things you ever heard. He told me, coming home, that he hoped the people saw him in the church, because he was a cripple, and it might be pleasant to them to remember upon Christmas Day, who made lame beggars walk, and blind men see.'

Bob's voice was tremulous when he told them this, and trembled more when he said that Tiny Tim was growing strong and hearty.

His active little crutch was heard upon the floor, and back came Tiny Tim before another word was spoken, escorted by his brother and sister to his stool beside the fire; and while Bob, turning up his cuffs – as if, poor fellow, they were capable of being made more shabby – compounded some hot mixture in a jug with gin and lemons, and stirred it round and round and put it on the hob to simmer; Master Peter, and the two ubiquitous young Cratchits went to fetch the goose, with which they soon returned in high procession.

Such a bustle ensued that you might have thought a goose the rarest of all birds; a feathered phenomenon, to which a black swan was a matter of course; and in truth it was something very like it in that house. Mrs. Cratchit made the gravy (ready beforehand in a little saucepan) hissing hot; Master Peter mashed the potatoes with incredible vigour; Miss Belinda sweetened up the apple-sauce; Martha dusted the hot plates; Bob took Tiny Tim beside him in a tiny corner at the table; the two young Cratchits set chairs for everybody, not forgetting themselves, and mounting guard upon their posts, crammed spoons into their mouths, lest they should shriek for goose before their turn came to be helped. At last the dishes were set on, and grace was said. It was succeeded by a breathless pause, as Mrs. Cratchit, looking slowly all along the carving-knife, prepared to plunge it in the breast; but when she did, and when the long expected gush of stuffing issued forth, one murmur of delight arose all round the board, and even Tiny Tim, excited by the two young Cratchits, beat on the table with the handle of his knife, and feebly cried Hurrah!

There never was such a goose. Bob said he didn't believe there ever was such a goose cooked. Its tenderness and flavour, size and cheapness, were the themes of universal admiration. Eked out by the apple-sauce and mashed potatoes, it was a sufficient dinner for the whole family; indeed, as Mrs. Cratchit said with great delight (surveying one small atom of a bone upon the dish), they hadn't ate it all at last! Yet every one had had enough, and the youngest Cratchits in particular, were steeped in sage and onion to the eyebrows! But now, the plates being changed by Miss Belinda,

Mrs. Cratchit left the room alone – too nervous to bear witnesses – to take the pudding up and bring it in.

Suppose it should not be done enough! Suppose it should break in turning out! Suppose somebody should have got over the wall of the back-yard, and stolen it, while they were merry with the goose: a supposition at which the two young Cratchits became livid! All sorts of horrors were supposed.

Hallo! A great deal of steam! The pudding was out of the copper. A smell like a washing-day! That was the cloth. A smell like an eating-house and a pastry cook's next door to each other, with a laundress's next door to that! That was the pudding. In half a minute Mrs. Cratchit entered: flushed, but smiling proudly: with the pudding, like a speckled cannon-ball, so hard and firm, blazing in half of half-a-quartern of ignited brandy, and bedight with Christmas holly stuck into the top.

Oh, a wonderful pudding! Bob Cratchit said, and calmly too, that he regarded it as the greatest success achieved by Mrs. Cratchit since their marriage. Mrs. Cratchit said that now the weight was off her mind, she would confess she had had her doubts about the quantity of flour. Everybody had something to say about it, but nobody said or thought it was at all a small pudding for a large family. It would have been flat heresy to do so. Any Cratchit would have blushed to hint at such a thing.

At last the dinner was all done, the cloth was cleared, the hearth swept, and the fire made up. The compound in the jug being tasted, and considered perfect, apples and oranges were put upon the table, and a shovel-full of chestnuts on the fire. Then all the Cratchit family drew round the hearth, in what Bob Cratchit called a circle, meaning half a one; and at Bob Cratchit's elbow stood the family display of glass; two tumblers, and a custard-cup without a handle.

These held the hot stuff from the jug, however, as well as golden goblets would have done; and Bob served it out with beaming looks, while the chestnuts on the fire sputtered and crackled noisily. Then Bob proposed:

'A Merry Christmas to us all, my dears. God bless us!'

Which all the family re-echoed.

'God bless us every one!' said Tiny Tim, the last of all.

He sat very close to his father's side upon his little stool. Bob held his withered little hand in his, as if he loved the child, and wished to keep him by his side, and dreaded that he might be taken from him.

'Spirit,' said Scrooge, with an interest he had never felt before, 'tell me if Tiny Tim will live.'

'I see a vacant seat,' replied the Ghost, 'in the poor chimney corner, and a crutch without an owner, carefully preserved. If these shadows remain unaltered by the Future, the child will die.'

'No, no,' said Scrooge. 'Oh, no, kind Spirit! say he will be spared.'

'If these shadows remain unaltered by the Future, none other of my race,' returned the Ghost, 'will find him here. What then? If he be like to die, he had better do it, and decrease the surplus population.'

Scrooge hung his head to hear his own words quoted by the Spirit, and was overcome with penitence and grief.

'Man,' said the Ghost, 'if man you be in heart, not adamant, forbear that wicked cant until you have discovered What the surplus is, and Where it is. Will you decide what men shall live, what men shall die? It may be, that in the sight of Heaven, you are more worthless and less fit to live than millions like this poor man's child. Oh God! to hear the Insect on the leaf pronouncing on the too much life among his hungry brothers in the dust!'

Scrooge bent before the Ghost's rebuke, and trembling cast his eyes upon the ground. But he raised them speedily, on hearing his own name.

'Mr. Scrooge!' said Bob; 'I'll give you Mr. Scrooge, the Founder of the Feast!'

'The Founder of the Feast indeed!' cried Mrs. Cratchit, reddening. 'I wish I had him here. I'd give him a piece of my mind to feast upon, and I hope he'd have a good appetite for it.'

'My dear,' said Bob, 'the children; Christmas Day.'

'It should be Christmas Day, I am sure,' said she, 'on which one drinks the health of such an odious, stingy, hard, unfeeling man as Mr. Scrooge. You know he is, Robert! Nobody knows it better than you do, poor fellow!'

'My dear,' was Bob's mild answer, 'Christmas Day.'

'I'll drink his health for your sake and the Day's,' said Mrs. Cratchit, 'not for his. Long life to him! A merry Christmas and a happy new year! – he'll be very merry and very happy, I have no doubt!'

The children drank the toast after her. It was the first of their proceedings which had no heartiness in it. Tiny Tim drank it last of all, but he didn't care twopence for it.

Scrooge was the Ogre of the family. The mention of his name cast a dark shadow on the party, which was not dispelled for full five minutes.

After it had passed away, they were ten times merrier than before, from the mere relief of Scrooge the Baleful being done with. Bob Cratchit told them how he had a situation in his eye for Master Peter, which would bring in, if obtained, full five-and-sixpence weekly. The two young Cratchits laughed tremendously at the idea of Peter's being a man of business; and Peter himself looked thoughtfully at the fire from between his collars, as if he were deliberating what particular investments he should favour when he came into the receipt of that bewildering income. Martha, who was a poor apprentice at a milliner's, then told them what kind of work she had to do, and how many hours she worked at a stretch, and how she meant to lie a-bed to-morrow morning for a good long rest; to-morrow being a holiday she passed at home. Also how she had seen a countess and a lord some days before, and how the lord 'was much about as tall as Peter'; at which Peter pulled up his collars so high that you couldn't have seen his head if you had been there. All this time the chestnuts and the jug went round and round; and bye and bye they had a song, about a lost child travelling in the snow, from Tiny Tim; who had a plaintive little voice, and sang it very well indeed.

There was nothing of high mark in this. They were not a handsome family; they were not well dressed; their shoes were far from being waterproof; their clothes were scanty; and Peter might have known, and very likely did, the inside of a pawnbroker's. But they were happy, grateful, pleased with one another, and contented with the time; and when they faded, and looked happier yet in the bright sprinklings of the Spirit's torch at parting, Scrooge had his eye upon them, and especially on Tiny Tim, until the last.

By this time it was getting dark, and snowing pretty heavily; and as Scrooge and the Spirit went along the streets, the brightness of the roaring fires in kitchens, parlours, and all sorts of rooms, was wonderful. Here, the flickering of the blaze showed preparations for a cosy dinner, with hot plates baking through and through before the fire, and deep red curtains, ready to be drawn, to shut out cold and darkness. There, all the children of the house were running out into the snow to meet their married sisters, brothers, cousins, uncles, aunts, and be the first to greet them. Here, again, were shadows on the window-blind of guests assembling; and there a group of handsome girls, all hooded and fur-booted, and all chattering at once, tripped lightly off to some near neighbour's house; where, woe upon the single man who saw them enter – artful witches: well they knew it – in a glow!

But if you had judged from the numbers of people on their way to friendly gatherings, you might have thought that no one was at home to give them welcome when they got there, instead of every house expecting company, and piling up its fires half-chimney high. Blessings on it, how the Ghost exulted! How it bared its breadth of breast, and opened its capacious palm, and floated on, outpouring, with a generous hand, its bright and harmless mirth on everything within its reach! The very lamplighter, who ran on before, dotting the dusky street with specks of light, and who was dressed to spend the evening somewhere, laughed out loudly as the Spirit passed: though little kenned the lamplighter that he had any company but Christmas!

And now, without a word of warning from the Ghost, they stood upon a bleak and desert moor, where monstrous masses of rude stone were cast about, as though it were the burial-place of giants; and water spread itself wheresoever it listed – or would have done so, but for the frost that held it prisoner; and nothing grew but moss and furze, and coarse rank grass. Down in the west the setting sun had left a streak of fiery red, which glared upon the desolation for an instant, like a sullen eye, and frowning lower, lower, lower yet, was lost in the thick gloom of darkest night.

'What place is this?' asked Scrooge.

'A place where Miners live, who labour in the bowels of the earth,' returned the Spirit. 'But they know me. See!'

A light shone from the window of a hut, and swiftly they advanced towards it. Passing through the wall of mud and stone, they found a cheerful company assembled round a glowing fire. An old, old man and woman, with their children and their children's children, and another generation beyond that, all decked out gaily in their holiday attire. The old man, in a voice that seldom rose above the howling of the wind upon the barren waste, was singing them a Christmas song; it had been a very old song when he was a boy; and from time to time they all joined in the chorus. So surely as they raised their voices, the old man got quite blithe and loud; and so surely as they stopped, his vigour sang again.

The Spirit did not tarry here, but bade Scrooge hold his robe, and passing on above the moor, sped whither? Not to sea? To sea. To Scrooge's horror, looking back, he saw the last of the land, a frightful range of rocks, behind them; and his ears were deafened by the thundering of water, as it rolled and roared, and raged among the dreadful caverns it had worn, and fiercely tried to undermine the earth.

Built upon a dismal reef of sunken rocks, some league or so from shore, on which the waters chafed and dashed, the wild year through, there stood a solitary lighthouse. Great heaps of sea-weed clung to its base, and storm-birds – born of the wind one might suppose, as sea-weed of the water – rose and fell about it, like the waves they skimmed.

But even here, two men who watched the light had made a fire, that through the loophole in the thick stone wall shed out a ray of brightness on the awful sea. Joining their horny hands over the rough table at which they sat, they wished each other Merry Christmas in their can of grog; and one of them: the elder, too, with his face all damaged and scarred with hard weather, as the figure-head of an old ship might be: struck up a sturdy song that was like a Gale in itself.

Again the Ghost sped on, above the black and heaving sea – on, on – until, being far away, as he told Scrooge, from any shore, they lighted on a ship. They stood beside the helmsman at the wheel, the look-out in the bow, the officers who had the watch; dark, ghostly figures in their several stations; but every man among them hummed a Christmas tune, or had a Christmas thought, or spoke below his breath to his companion of some bygone Christmas Day, with homeward hopes belonging to it. And every man on board, waking or sleeping, good or bad, had had a kinder word for another on that day than on any day in the year; and had shared to some extent in its festivities; and had remembered those he cared for at a distance, and had known that they delighted to remember him.

It was a great surprise to Scrooge, while listening to the moaning of the wind, and thinking what a solemn thing it was to move on through the lonely darkness over an unknown abyss, whose depths were secrets as profound as Death: it was a great surprise to Scrooge, while thus engaged, to hear a hearty laugh. It was a much greater surprise to Scrooge to recognise it as his own nephew's, and to find himself in a bright, dry, gleaming room, with the Spirit standing smiling by his side, and looking at that same nephew with approving affability!

'Ha, ha!' laughed Scrooge's nephew. 'Ha, ha, ha!'

If you should happen, by any unlikely chance, to know a man more blest in a laugh than Scrooge's nephew, all I can say is, I should like to know him too. Introduce him to me, and I'll cultivate his acquaintance.

It is a fair, even-handed, noble adjustment of things, that while there is infection in disease and sorrow, there is nothing in the world so irresistibly contagious as laughter and good-humour. When Scrooge's nephew laughed in this way: holding his sides, rolling his head, and twisting his face into the most extravagant contortions: Scrooge's niece, by marriage, laughed as heartily as he. And their assembled friends being not a bit behindhand, roared out, lustily.

'Ha, ha! Ha, ha, ha, ha!'

'He said that Christmas was a humbug, as I live!' cried Scrooge's nephew. 'He believed it too!'

'More shame for him, Fred!' said Scrooge's niece, indignantly. Bless those women; they never do anything by halves. They are always in earnest.

She was very pretty: exceedingly pretty. With a dimpled, surprised-looking, capital face; a ripe little mouth, that seemed made to be kissed – as no doubt it was; all kinds of good little dots about her chin, that melted into one another when she laughed; and the sunniest pair of eyes you ever saw in any little creature's head. Altogether she was what you would have called provoking, you know; but satisfactory too. Oh, perfectly satisfactory!

'He's a comical old fellow,' said Scrooge's nephew, 'that's the truth: and not so pleasant as he might be. However, his offences carry their own punishment, and I have nothing to say against him.'

'I'm sure he is very rich, Fred,' hinted Scrooge's niece. 'At least you always tell *me* so.'

'What of that, my dear!' said Scrooge's nephew. 'His wealth is of no use to him. He don't do any good with it. He don't make himself comfortable with it. He hasn't the satisfaction of thinking – ha, ha, ha! – that he is ever going to benefit Us with it.'

'I have no patience with him,' observed Scrooge's niece. Scrooge's niece's sisters, and all the other ladies, expressed the same opinion.

'Oh, I have!' said Scrooge's nephew. 'I am sorry for him; I couldn't be angry with him if I tried. Who suffers by his ill whims. Himself, always. Here, he takes it into his head to dislike us, and he won't come and dine with us. What's the consequence? He don't lose much of a dinner.'

'Indeed, I think he loses a very good dinner,' interrupted Scrooge's niece. Everybody else said the same, and they must be allowed to have been competent judges, because they had just had dinner; and, with the dessert upon the table, were clustered round the fire, by lamplight.

'Well! I'm very glad to hear it,' said Scrooge's nephew, 'because I haven't great faith in these young housekeepers. What do *you* say, Topper?'

Topper had clearly got his eye upon one of Scrooge's niece's sisters, for he answered that a bachelor was a wretched outcast, who had no right to express an opinion on the subject. Whereat Scrooge's niece's sister – the plump one with the lace tucker: not the one with the roses – blushed.

'Do go on, Fred,' said Scrooge's niece, clapping her hands. 'He never finishes what he begins to say! He is such a ridiculous fellow!'

Scrooge's nephew revelled in another laugh, and as it was impossible to keep the infection off; though the plump sister tried hard to do it with aromatic vinegar; his example was unanimously followed.

'I was only going to say,' said Scrooge's nephew, 'that the consequence of his taking a dislike to us, and not making merry with us, is, as I think, that he loses some pleasant moments, which could do him no harm. I am sure he loses pleasanter companions than he can find in his own thoughts, either in his mouldy old office, or his dusty chambers. I mean to give him the same chance every year, whether he likes it or not, for I pity him. He may rail at Christmas till he dies, but he can't help thinking better of it – I defy him – if he finds me going there, in good temper, year after year, and saying Uncle Scrooge, how are you? If it only puts him in the vein to leave his poor clerk fifty pounds, *that's* something; and I think I shook him, yesterday.'

It was their turn to laugh now, at the notion of his shaking Scrooge. But being thoroughly good-natured, and not much caring what they laughed at, so that they laughed at any rate, he encouraged them in their merriment, and passed the bottle, joyously.

After tea, they had some music. For they were a musical family, and knew what they were about, when they sung a Glee or Catch, I can assure you: especially Topper, who could growl away in the bass like a good one, and never swell the large veins in his forehead, or get red in the face over it. Scrooge's niece played well upon the harp; and played among other tunes a simple little air (a mere nothing: you might learn to whistle it in two minutes), which had been familiar to the child who fetched Scrooge from the boarding-school, as he had been reminded by the Ghost of Christmas Past.

When this strain of music sounded, all the things that Ghost had shown him, came upon his mind; he softened more and more; and thought that if he could have listened to it often, years ago, he might have cultivated the kindnesses of life for his own happiness with his own hands, without resorting to the sexton's spade that buried Jacob Marley.

But they didn't devote the whole evening to music. After a while they played at forfeits; for it is good to be children sometimes, and never better than at Christmas, when its mighty Founder was a child himself. Stop! There was first a game at blindman's buff. Of course there was. And I no more believe Topper was really blind than I believe he had eyes in his boots. My opinion is, that it was a done thing between him and Scrooge's nephew; and that the Ghost of Christmas Present knew it. The way he went after that plump sister in the lace tucker, was an outrage on the credulity of human nature. Knocking down the fire-irons, tumbling over the chairs, bumping against the piano, smothering himself among the curtains, wherever she went, there went he. He always knew where the plump sister was. He wouldn't catch anybody else. If you had fallen up against him, as some of them did, and stood there; he would have made a feint of endeavouring to seize you, which would have been an affront to your understanding; and would instantly have sidled off in the direction of the plump sister. She often cried out that it wasn't fair; and it really was not. But when at last, he caught her; when, in spite of all her silken rustlings, and her rapid flutterings past him, he got her into a corner whence there was no escape; then his conduct was the most execrable. For his pretending not to know her; his pretending that it was necessary to touch her head-dress, and further to assure himself of her identity by pressing a certain ring upon her finger, and a certain chain about her neck; was vile, monstrous! No doubt she told him her opinion of it, when, another blind-man being in office, they were so very confidential together, behind the curtains.

Scrooge's niece was not one of the blind-man's buff party, but was made comfortable with a large chair and a footstool, in a snug corner, where the Ghost and Scrooge were close behind her. But she joined in the forfeits, and loved her love to admiration with all the letters of the alphabet. Likewise at the game of How, When, and Where, she was very great, and to the secret joy of Scrooge's nephew, beat her sisters hollow: though they were sharp girls too, as Topper could have told you. There might have been twenty people there, young and old, but they all played, and so did Scrooge;

for, wholly forgetting the interest he had in what was going on, that his voice made no sound in their ears, he sometimes came out with his guess quite loud, and very often guessed quite right, too; for the sharpest needle, best Whitechapel, warranted not to cut in the eye, was not sharper than Scrooge; blunt as he took it in his head to be.

The Ghost was greatly pleased to find him in this mood, and looked upon him with such favour, that he begged like a boy to be allowed to stay until the guests departed. But this the Spirit said could not be done.

'Here is a new game,' said Scrooge. 'One half hour, Spirit, only one!'

It was a Game called Yes and No, where Scrooge's nephew had to think of something, and the rest must find out what; he only answering to their questions yes or no as the case was. The brisk fire of questioning to which he was exposed, elicited from him that he was thinking of an animal, a live animal, rather a disagreeable animal, a savage animal, an animal that growled and grunted sometimes, and talked sometimes, and lived in London, and walked about the streets, and wasn't made a show of, and wasn't led by anybody, and didn't live in a menagerie, and was never killed in a market, and was not a horse, or an ass, or a cow, or a bull, or a tiger, or a dog, or a pig, or a cat, or a bear. At every fresh question that was put to him, this nephew burst into a fresh roar of laughter; and was so inexpressibly tickled, that he was obliged to get up off the sofa and stamp. At last the plump sister, falling into a similar state, cried out:

'I have found it out! I know what it is, Fred. I know what it is!'

'What is it?' cried Fred.

'It's your Uncle Scrooge!'

Which it certainly was. Admiration was the universal sentiment, though some objected that the reply to 'Is it a bear?' ought to have been 'Yes;' inasmuch as an answer in the negative was sufficient to have diverted their thoughts from Mr. Scrooge, supposing they had ever had any tendency that way.

'He has given us plenty of merriment, I am sure,' said Fred, 'and it would be ungrateful not to drink his health. Here is a glass of mulled wine ready to our hand at the moment; and I say, "Uncle Scrooge!"'

'Well! Uncle Scrooge!' they cried.

'A Merry Christmas and a Happy New Year to the old man, whatever he is!' said Scrooge's nephew. 'He wouldn't take it from me, but may he have it, nevertheless. Uncle Scrooge!'

Uncle Scrooge had imperceptibly become so gay and light of heart, that he would have pledged the unconscious company in return, and thanked them in an inaudible speech, if the Ghost had given him time. But the whole scene passed off in the breath of the last word spoken by his nephew; and he and the Spirit were again upon their travels.

Much they saw, and far they went, and many homes they visited, but always with a happy end. The Spirit stood beside sick beds, and they were cheerful; on foreign lands, and they were close at home; by struggling men, and they were patient in their greater hope; by poverty, and it was rich. In almshouse, hospital, and jail, in misery's every refuge, where vain man in his little brief authority had not made fast the door, and barred the Spirit out, he left his blessing, and taught Scrooge his precepts.

It was a long night, if it were only a night; but Scrooge had his doubts of this, because the Christmas Holidays appeared to be condensed into the space of time they passed together. It was strange, too, that while Scrooge remained unaltered in his outward form, the Ghost grew older, clearly older. Scrooge had observed this change, but never spoke of it, until they left a children's Twelfth Night party, when, looking at the Spirit as they stood together in an open place, he noticed that its hair was grey.

'Are spirits' lives so short?' asked Scrooge.

'My life upon this globe, is very brief,' replied the Ghost. 'It ends to-night.'

'To-night!' cried Scrooge.

'To-night at midnight. Hark! The time is drawing near.'

The chimes were ringing the three quarters past eleven at that moment.

'Forgive me if I am not justified in what I ask,' said Scrooge, looking intently at the Spirit's robe, 'but I see something strange, and not belonging to yourself, protruding from your skirts. Is it a foot or a claw!'

'It might be a claw, for the flesh there is upon it,' was the Spirit's sorrowful reply. 'Look here.'

From the foldings of its robe, it brought two children; wretched, abject, frightful, hideous, miserable. They knelt down at its feet, and clung upon the outside of its garment.

'Oh, Man! look here. Look, look, down here!' exclaimed the Ghost.

They were a boy and girl. Yellow, meagre, ragged, scowling, wolfish; but prostrate, too, in their humility. Where graceful youth should have filled their features out, and touched them with its freshest tints, a stale and shrivelled hand, like that of age, had pinched, and twisted them, and pulled them into shreds. Where angels might have sat enthroned, devils lurked, and glared out menacing. No change, no degradation, no perversion of humanity, in any grade, through all the mysteries of wonderful creation, has monsters half so horrible and dread.

Scrooge started back, appalled. Having them shown to him in this way, he tried to say they were fine children, but the words choked themselves, rather than be parties to a lie of such enormous magnitude.

'Spirit! are they yours?' Scrooge could say no more.

'They are Man's,' said the Spirit, looking down upon them. 'And they cling to me, appealing from their fathers. This boy is Ignorance. This girl is Want. Beware them both, and all of their degree, but most of all beware this boy, for on his brow I see that written which is Doom, unless the writing be erased. Deny it!' cried the Spirit, stretching out its hand towards the city. 'Slander those who tell it ye. Admit it for your factious purposes, and make it worse. And abide the end!'

'Have they no refuge or resource?' cried Scrooge.

'Are there no prisons?' said the Spirit, turning on him for the last time with his own words. 'Are there no workhouses?'

The bell struck twelve.

Scrooge looked about him for the Ghost, and saw it not. As the last stroke ceased to vibrate, he remembered the prediction of old Jacob Marley, and lifting up his eyes, beheld a solemn Phantom, draped and hooded, coming, like a mist along the ground, towards him.

STAVE 4

The Last of the Spirits

The Phantom slowly, gravely, silently, approached. When it came near him, Scrooge bent down upon his knee; for in the very air through which this Spirit moved it seemed to scatter gloom and mystery.

It was shrouded in a deep black garment, which concealed its head, its face, its form, and left nothing of it visible save one outstretched hand. But for this it would have been difficult to detach its figure from the night, and separate it from the darkness by which it was surrounded.

He felt that it was tall and stately when it came beside him, and that its mysterious presence filled him with a solemn dread. He knew no more, for the Spirit neither spoke nor moved.

'I am in the presence of the Ghost of Christmas Yet To Come?' said Scrooge.

The Spirit answered not, but pointed downward with its hand.

'You are about to show me shadows of the things that have not happened, but will happen in the time before us,' Scrooge pursued. 'Is that so, Spirit?'

The upper portion of the garment was contracted for an instant in its folds, as if the Spirit had inclined its head. That was the only answer he received.

Although well used to ghostly company by this time, Scrooge feared the silent shape so much that his legs trembled beneath him, and he found that he could hardly stand when he prepared to follow it. The Spirit paused a moment, as observing his condition, and giving him time to recover.

But Scrooge was all the worse for this. It thrilled him with a vague uncertain horror, to know that behind the dusky shroud, there were ghostly eyes intently fixed upon him, while he, though he stretched his own to the utmost, could see nothing but a spectral hand and one great heap of black.

'Ghost of the Future!' he exclaimed, 'I fear you more than any Spectre I have seen. But, as I know your purpose is to do me good, and as I hope to live to be another man from what I was, I am prepared to bear you company, and do it with a thankful heart. Will you not speak to me?'

It gave him no reply. The hand was pointed straight before them.

'Lead on!' said Scrooge. 'Lead on! The night is waning fast, and it is precious time to me, I know. Lead on, Spirit!'

The Phantom moved away as it had come towards him. Scrooge followed in the shadow of its dress, which bore him up, he thought, and carried him along.

They scarcely seemed to enter the city; for the city rather seemed to spring up about them, and encompass them of its own act. But there they were, in the heart of it; on 'Change, amongst the merchants; who hurried up and down, and chinked the money in their pockets, and conversed in groups, and looked at their watches, and trifled thoughtfully with their great gold seals; and so forth, as Scrooge had seen them often.

The Spirit stopped beside one little knot of business men. Observing that the hand was pointed to them, Scrooge advanced to listen to their talk.

'No,' said a great fat man with a monstrous chin, 'I don't know much about it, either way. I only know he's dead.'

'When did he die?' inquired another.

'Last night, I believe.'

'Why, what was the matter with him?' asked a third, taking a vast quantity of snuff out of a very large snuff-box. 'I thought he'd never die.'

'God knows,' said the first, with a yawn.

'What has he done with his money?' asked a red-faced gentleman with a pendulous excrescence on the end of his nose, that shook like the gills of a turkey-cock.

'I haven't heard,' said the man with the large chin, yawning again. 'Left it to his Company, perhaps. He hasn't left it to *me*. That's all I know.'

This pleasantry was received with a general laugh.

'It's likely to be a very cheap funeral,' said the same speaker; 'for upon my life I don't know of anybody to go to it. Suppose we make up a party and volunteer?'

'I don't mind going if a lunch is provided,' observed the gentleman with the excrescence on his nose. 'But I must be fed, if I make one.'

Another laugh.

'Well, I am the most disinterested among you, after all,' said the first speaker, 'for I never wear black gloves, and I never eat lunch. But I'll offer to go, if anybody else will. When I come to think of it, I'm not at all sure that I wasn't his most particular friend; for we used to stop and speak whenever we met. Bye, bye!'

Speakers and listeners strolled away, and mixed with other groups. Scrooge knew the men, and looked towards the Spirit for an explanation.

The Phantom glided on into a street. Its finger pointed to two persons meeting. Scrooge listened again, thinking that the explanation might lie here.

He knew these men, also, perfectly. They were men of business: very wealthy, and of great importance. He had made a point always of standing well in their esteem: in a business point of view, that is; strictly in a business point of view.

'How are you?' said one.

'How are you?' returned the other.

'Well!' said the first. 'Old Scratch has got his own at last, hey?'

'So I am told,' returned the second. 'Cold, isn't it?'

'Seasonable for Christmas time. You're not a skater, I suppose?'

'No. No. Something else to think of. Good morning!'

Not another word. That was their meeting, their conversation, and their parting.

Scrooge was at first inclined to be surprised that the Spirit should attach importance to conversations apparently so trivial; but feeling assured that they must have some hidden purpose, he set himself to consider what it was likely to be. They could scarcely be supposed to have any bearing on the death of Jacob, his old partner, for that was Past, and this Ghost's province was the Future. Nor could he think of any one immediately connected with himself, to whom he could apply them. But nothing doubting that to whomsoever they applied they had some latent moral for his own improvement, he resolved to treasure up every word he heard, and everything he saw; and especially to observe the shadow of himself when it appeared. For he had an expectation that the conduct of his future self would give him the clue he missed, and would render the solution of these riddles easy.

He looked about in that very place for his own image; but another man stood in his accustomed corner, and though the clock pointed to his usual time of day for being there, he saw no likeness of himself among the multitudes that poured in through the Porch. It gave him little surprise, however; for he had been revolving in his mind a change of life, and thought and hoped he saw his new-born resolutions carried out in this.

Quiet and dark, beside him stood the Phantom, with its outstretched hand. When he roused himself from his thoughtful quest, he fancied from the turn of the hand, and its situation in reference to himself, that the Unseen Eyes were looking at him keenly. It made him shudder, and feel very cold.

They left the busy scene, and went into an obscure part of the town, where Scrooge had never penetrated before, although he recognised its situation, and its bad repute. The ways were foul and narrow; the shops and houses wretched; the people half-naked, drunken, slipshod, ugly. Alleys and archways, like so many cesspools, disgorged their offences of smell, and dirt, and life, upon the straggling streets; and the whole quarter reeked with crime, with filth, and misery.

Far in this den of infamous resort, there was a low-browed, beetling shop, below a pent-house roof, where iron, old rags, bottles, bones, and greasy offal, were bought.

Upon the floor within, were piled up heaps of rusty keys, nails, chains, hinges, files, scales, weights, and refuse iron of all kinds. Secrets that few would like to scrutinise were bred and hidden in mountains of unseemly rags, masses of corrupted fat, and sepulchres of bones. Sitting in among the wares he dealt in, by a charcoal-stove, made of old bricks, was a grey-haired rascal, nearly seventy years of age; who had screened himself from the cold air without, by a frousy curtaining of miscellaneous tatters, hung upon a line; and smoked his pipe in all the luxury of calm retirement.

Scrooge and the Phantom came into the presence of this man, just as a woman with a heavy bundle slunk into the shop. But she had scarcely entered, when another woman, similarly laden, came in too; and she was closely followed by a man in faded black, who was no less startled by the sight of them, than they had been upon the recognition of each other. After a short period of blank astonishment, in which the old man with the pipe had joined them, they all three burst into a laugh.

'Let the charwoman alone to be the first!' cried she who had entered first. 'Let the laundress alone to be the second; and let the undertaker's man alone to be the third. Look here, old Joe, here's a chance! If we haven't all three met here without meaning it.'

'You couldn't have met in a better place,' said old Joe, removing his pipe from his mouth. 'Come into the parlour. You were made free of it long ago, you know; and the other two ain't strangers. Stop till I shut the door of the shop. Ah! How it skreeks! There ain't such a rusty bit of metal in the place as its own hinges, I believe; and I'm sure there's no such old bones here, as mine. Ha, ha! We're all suitable to our calling, we're well matched. Come into the parlour. Come into the parlour.'

The parlour was the space behind the screen of rags. The old man raked the fire together with an old stair-rod, and having trimmed his smoky lamp (for it was night), with the stem of his pipe, put it in his mouth again.

While he did this, the woman who had already spoken threw her bundle on the floor, and sat down in a flaunting manner on a stool; crossing her elbows on her knees, and looking with a bold defiance at the other two.

'What odds then! What odds, Mrs. Dilber?' said the woman. 'Every person has a right to take care of themselves. *He* always did!'

'That's true, indeed!' said the laundress. 'No man more so.'

'Why then, don't stand staring as if you was afraid, woman; who's the wiser? We're not going to pick holes in each other's coats, I suppose?'

'No, indeed!' said Mrs. Dilber and the man together. 'We should hope not.'

'Very well, then!' cried the woman. 'That's enough. Who's the worse for the loss of a few things like these? Not a dead man, I suppose.'

'No, indeed,' said Mrs. Dilber, laughing.

'If he wanted to keep them after he was dead, a wicked old screw,' pursued the woman, 'why wasn't he natural in his lifetime? If he had been, he'd have had somebody to look after him when he was struck with Death, instead of lying gasping out his last there, alone by himself.'

'It's the truest word that ever was spoke,' said Mrs Dilber. 'It's a judgment on him.'

'I wish it was a little heavier one,' replied the woman; 'and it should have been, you may depend upon it, if I could have laid my hands on anything else. Open that bundle, old Joe, and let me know the value of it. Speak out plain. I'm not afraid to be the first, nor afraid for them to see it. We know pretty well that we were helping ourselves, before we met here, I believe. It's no sin. Open the bundle, Joe.'

But the gallantry of her friends would not allow of this; and the man in faded black, mounting the breach first, produced *his* plunder. It was not extensive. A seal or two, a pencil-case, a pair of sleeve-buttons, and a brooch of no great value, were all. They were severally examined and appraised by old Joe, who chalked the sums he was disposed to give for each, upon the wall, and added them up into a total when he found there was nothing more to come.

'That's your account,' said Joe, 'and I wouldn't give another sixpence, if I was to be boiled for not doing it. Who's next?'

Mrs. Dilber was next. Sheets and towels, a little wearing apparel, two old-fashioned silver teaspoons, a pair of sugar-tongs, and a few boots. Her account was stated on the wall in the same manner.

'I always give too much to ladies. It's a weakness of mine, and that's the way I ruin myself,' said old Joe. 'That's your account. If you asked me for another penny, and made it an open question, I'd repent of being so liberal and knock off half-a-crown.'

'And now undo *my* bundle, Joe,' said the first woman.

Joe went down on his knees for the greater convenience of opening it, and having unfastened a great many knots, dragged out a large and heavy roll of some dark stuff.

'What do you call this?' said Joe. 'Bed-curtains!'

'Ah!' returned the woman, laughing and leaning forward on her crossed arms.

'Bed-curtains!'

'You don't mean to say you took them down, rings and all, with him lying there?' said Joe.

'Yes I do,' replied the woman. 'Why not?'

'You were born to make your fortune,' said Joe, 'and you'll certainly do it.'

'I certainly shan't hold my hand, when I can get anything in it by reaching it out, for the sake of such a man as He was, I promise you, Joe,' returned the woman coolly. 'Don't drop that oil upon the blankets, now.'

'His blankets?' asked Joe.

'Whose else's do you think.' replied the woman. 'He isn't likely to take cold without 'em, I dare say.'

'I hope he didn't die of anything catching? Eh?' said old Joe, stopping in his work, and looking up.

'Don't you be afraid of that,' returned the woman. 'I an't so fond of his company that I'd loiter about him for such things, if he did. Ah! you may look through that shirt till your eyes ache; but you won't find a hole in it, nor a threadbare place. It's the best he had, and a fine one too. They'd have wasted it, if it hadn't been for me.'

'What do you call wasting of it?' asked old Joe.

'Putting it on him to be buried in, to be sure,' replied the woman with a laugh. 'Somebody was fool enough to do it, but I took it off again. If calico an't good enough for such a purpose, it isn't good enough for anything. It's quite as becoming to the body. He can't look uglier than he did in that one.'

Scrooge listened to this dialogue in horror. As they sat grouped about their spoil, in the scanty light afforded by the old man's lamp, he viewed them with a detestation and disgust, which could hardly have been greater, though they had been obscene demons, marketing the corpse itself.

'Ha, ha!' laughed the same woman, when old Joe, producing a flannel bag with money in it, told out their several gains upon the ground. 'This is the end of it, you see! He frightened every one away from him when he was alive, to profit us when he was dead! Ha, ha, ha!'

'Spirit!' said Scrooge, shuddering from head to foot. 'I see, I see. The case of this unhappy man might be my own. My life tends that way, now. Merciful Heaven, what is this!'

He recoiled in terror, for the scene had changed, and now he almost touched a bed: a bare, uncurtained bed: on which, beneath a ragged sheet, there lay a something covered up, which, though it was dumb, announced itself in awful language.

The room was very dark, too dark to be observed with any accuracy, though Scrooge glanced round it in obedience to a secret impulse, anxious to know what kind of room it was. A pale light, rising in the outer air, fell straight upon the bed; and on it, plundered and bereft, unwatched, unwept, uncared for, was the body of this man.

Scrooge glanced towards the Phantom. Its steady hand was pointed to the head. The cover was so carelessly adjusted that the slightest raising of it, the motion of a finger upon Scrooge's part, would have disclosed the face. He thought of it, felt how easy it would be to do, and longed to do it; but had no more power to withdraw the veil than to dismiss the spectre at his side.

Oh cold, cold, rigid, dreadful Death, set up thine altar here, and dress it with such terrors as thou hast at thy command: for this is thy dominion. But of the loved, revered, and honoured head, thou canst not turn one hair to thy dread purposes, or make one feature odious. It is not that the hand is heavy and will fall down when released; it is not that the heart and pulse are still; but that the hand WAS open, generous, and true; the heart brave, warm, and tender; and the pulse a man's. Strike, Shadow, strike! And see his good deeds springing from the wound, to sow the world with life immortal!

No voice pronounced these words in Scrooge's ears, and yet he heard them when he looked upon the bed. He thought, if this man could be raised up now, what would be his foremost thoughts? Avarice, hard-dealing, griping cares. They have brought him to a rich end, truly!

He lay, in the dark empty house, with not a man, a woman, or a child, to say that he was kind to me in this or that, and for the memory of one kind word I will be kind to him. A cat was tearing at the door, and there was a sound of gnawing rats beneath the hearth-stone. What *they* wanted in the room of death, and why they were so restless and disturbed, Scrooge did not dare to think.

'Spirit!' he said, 'this is a fearful place. In leaving it, I shall not leave its lesson, trust me. Let us go!'

Still the Ghost pointed with an unmoved finger to the head.

'I understand you,' Scrooge returned, 'and I would do it, if I could. But I have not the power, Spirit. I have not the power.'

Again it seemed to look upon him.

'If there is any person in the town, who feels emotion caused by this man's death,' said Scrooge quite agonized, 'show that person to me, Spirit, I beseech you!'

The phantom spread its dark robe before him for a moment, like a wing; and withdrawing it, revealed a room by daylight, where a mother and her children were.

She was expecting some one, and with anxious eagerness; for she walked up and down the room; started at every sound; looked out from the window; glanced at the clock; tried, but in vain, to work with her needle; and could hardly bear the voices of the children in their play.

At length the long-expected knock was heard. She hurried to the door, and met her husband; a man whose face was care-worn and depressed, though he was young. There was a remarkable expression in it now; a kind of serious delight of which he felt ashamed, and which he struggled to repress.

He sat down to the dinner that had been hoarding for him by the fire; and when she asked him faintly what news (which was not until after a long silence), he appeared embarrassed how to answer.

'Is it good,' she said, 'or bad?' – to help him.

'Bad,' he answered.

'We are quite ruined?'

'No. There is hope yet, Caroline.'

'If *he* relents,' she said, amazed, 'there is! Nothing is past hope, if such a miracle has happened.'

'He is past relenting,' said her husband. 'He is dead.'

She was a mild and patient creature if her face spoke truth; but she was thankful in her soul to hear it, and she said so, with clasped hands. She prayed forgiveness the next moment, and was sorry; but the first was the emotion of her heart.

'What the half-drunken woman whom I told you of last night, said to me, when I tried to see him and obtain a week's delay; and what I thought was a mere excuse to avoid me; turns out to have been quite true. He was not only very ill, but dying, then.'

'To whom will our debt be transferred?'

'I don't know. But before that time we shall be ready with the money; and even though we were not, it would be a bad fortune indeed to find so merciless a creditor in his successor. We may sleep to-night with light hearts, Caroline!'

Yes. Soften it as they would, their hearts were lighter. The children's faces hushed, and clustered round to hear what they so little understood, were brighter; and it was a happier house for this man's death! The only emotion that the Ghost could show him, caused by the event, was one of pleasure.

'Let me see some tenderness connected with a death,' said Scrooge; 'or that dark chamber, Spirit, which we left just now, will be for ever present to me.'

The Ghost conducted him through several streets familiar to his feet; and as they went along, Scrooge looked here and there to find himself, but nowhere was he to be seen. They entered poor Bob Cratchit's house; the dwelling he had visited before; and found the mother and the children seated round the fire.

Quiet. Very quiet. The noisy little Cratchits were as still as statues in one corner, and sat looking up at Peter, who had a book before him. The mother and her daughters were engaged in sewing. But surely they were very quiet!

"And He took a child, and set him in the midst of them."

Where had Scrooge heard those words? He had not dreamed them. The boy must have read them out, as he and the Spirit crossed the threshold. Why did he not go on?

The mother laid her work upon the table, and put her hand up to her face.

'The colour hurts my eyes,' she said.

The colour? Ah, poor Tiny Tim!

'They're better now again,' said Cratchit's wife. 'It makes them weak by candle-light; and I wouldn't show weak eyes to your father when he comes home, for the world. It must be near his time.'

'Past it rather,' Peter answered, shutting up his book. 'But I think he has walked a little slower than he used, these few last evenings, mother.'

They were very quiet again. At last she said, and in a steady, cheerful voice, that only faltered once:

'I have known him walk with – I have known him walk with Tiny Tim upon his shoulder, very fast indeed.'

'And so have I,' cried Peter. 'Often.'

'And so have I!' exclaimed another. So had all.

'But he was very light to carry,' she resumed, intent upon her work, 'And his father loved him so, that it was no trouble – no trouble. And there is your father at the door!'

She hurried out to meet him; and little Bob in his comforter – he had need of it, poor fellow – came in. His tea was ready for him on the hob, and they all tried who should help him to it most. Then the two young Cratchits got upon his knees and laid, each child a little cheek, against his face, as if they said, 'Don't mind it, father. Don't be grieved!'

Bob was very cheerful with them, and spoke pleasantly to all the family. He looked at the work upon the table, and praised the industry and speed of Mrs. Cratchit and the girls. They would be done long before Sunday, he said.

'Sunday. You went to-day then, Robert?' said his wife.

'Yes, my dear,' returned Bob. 'I wish you could have gone. It would have done you good to see how green a place it is. But you'll see it often. I promised him that I would walk there on a Sunday. My little, little child!' cried Bob. 'My little child!'

He broke down all at once. He couldn't help it. If he could have helped it, he and his child would have been farther apart perhaps than they were.

He left the room, and went upstairs into the room above, which was lighted cheerfully, and hung with Christmas. There was a chair set close beside the child, and there were signs of some one having been there, lately. Poor Bob sat down in it, and when he had thought a little and composed himself, he kissed the little face. He was reconciled to what had happened, and went down again quite happy.

They drew about the fire, and talked; the girls and mother working still. Bob told them of the extraordinary kindness of Mr. Scrooge's nephew, whom he had scarcely seen but once, and who, meeting him in the street that day, and seeing that he looked a little – 'just a little down you know' said Bob, enquired what had happened to distress him. 'On which,' said Bob, 'for he is the pleasantest-spoken gentleman you ever heard, I told him. "I am heartily sorry for it, Mr. Cratchit," he said, "and heartily sorry for your good wife." By the bye, how he ever knew *that*, I don't know.'

'Know what, my dear?'

'Why, that you were a good wife,' replied Bob.

'Everybody knows that!' said Peter.

'Very well observed, my boy!' cried Bob. 'I hope they do. "Heartily sorry," he said, "for your good wife. If I can be of service to you in any way," he said, giving me his card, "that's where I live. Pray come to me." Now, it wasn't,' cried Bob, 'for the sake of anything he might be able to do for us, so much as for his kind way, that this was quite delightful. It really seemed as if he had known our Tiny Tim, and felt with us.'

'I'm sure he's a good soul!' said Mrs. Cratchit.

'You would be surer of it, my dear,' returned Bob, 'if you saw and spoke to him. I shouldn't be at all surprised, mark what I say, if he got Peter a better situation.'

'Only hear that, Peter,' said Mrs. Cratchit.

'And then,' cried one of the girls, 'Peter will be keeping company with some one, and setting up for himself.'

'Get along with you!' retorted Peter, grinning.

'It's just as likely as not,' said Bob, 'one of these days; though there's plenty of time for that, my dear. But however and whenever we part from one another, I am sure we shall none of us forget poor Tiny Tim – shall we – or this first parting that there was among us?'

'Never, father!' cried they all.

'And I know,' said Bob, 'I know, my dears, that when we recollect how patient and how mild he was; although he was a little, little child; we shall not quarrel easily among ourselves, and forget poor Tiny Tim in doing it.'

'No, never, father!' they all cried again.

'I am very happy,' said little Bob, 'I am very happy.'

Mrs. Cratchit kissed him, his daughters kissed him, the two young Cratchits kissed him, and Peter and himself shook hands. Spirit of Tiny Tim, thy childish essence was from God!

'Spectre,' said Scrooge, 'something informs me that our parting moment is at hand. I know it, but I know not how. Tell me what man that was whom we saw lying dead?'

The Ghost of Christmas Yet To Come conveyed him, as before – though at a different time, he thought: indeed, there seemed no order in these latter visions, save that they were in the Future – into the resorts of business men, but showed him not himself. Indeed, the Spirit did not stay for anything, but went straight on, as to the end just now desired, until besought by Scrooge to tarry for a moment.

'This court,' said Scrooge, 'through which we hurry now, is where my place of occupation is, and has been for a length of time. I see the house. Let me behold what I shall be, in days to come.'

The Spirit stopped; the hand was pointed elsewhere.

'The house is yonder,' Scrooge exclaimed. 'Why do you point away?'

The inexorable finger underwent no change.

Scrooge hastened to the window of his office, and looked in. It was an office still, but not his. The furniture was not the same, and the figure in the chair was not himself. The Phantom pointed as before.

He joined it once again, and wondering why and whither he had gone, accompanied it until they reached an iron gate. He paused to look round before entering.

A churchyard. Here, then, the wretched man whose name he had now to learn, lay underneath the ground. It was a worthy place. Walled in by houses; overrun by grass and weeds, the growth of vegetation's death, not life; choked up with too much burying; fat with repleted appetite. A worthy place!

The Spirit stood among the graves, and pointed down to One. He advanced towards it trembling. The Phantom was exactly as it had been, but he dreaded that he saw new meaning in its solemn shape.

'Before I draw nearer to that stone to which you point,' said Scrooge, 'answer me one question. Are these the shadows of the things that Will be, or are they shadows of things that May be, only?'

Still the Ghost pointed downward to the grave by which it stood.

'Men's courses will foreshadow certain ends, to which, if persevered in, they must lead,' said Scrooge. 'But if the courses be departed from, the ends will change. Say it is thus with what you show me!'

The Spirit was immovable as ever.

Scrooge crept towards it, trembling as he went; and following the finger, read upon the stone of the neglected grave his own name, EBENEZER SCROOGE.

'Am I that man who lay upon the bed?' he cried, upon his knees.

The finger pointed from the grave to him, and back again.

'No, Spirit! Oh no, no!'

The finger still was there

'Spirit!' he cried, tight clutching at its robe, 'hear me! I am not the man I was. I will not be the man I must have been but for this intercourse. Why show me this, if I am past all hope?'

For the first time the hand appeared to shake.

'Good Spirit,' he pursued, as down upon the ground he fell before it: 'Your nature intercedes for me, and pities me. Assure me that I yet may change these shadows you have shown me, by an altered life!'

The kind hand trembled.

'I will honour Christmas in my heart, and try to keep it all the year. I will live in the Past, the Present, and the Future. The Spirits of all Three shall strive within me. I will not shut out the lessons that they teach. Oh, tell me I may sponge away the writing on this stone!'

In his agony, he caught the spectral hand. It sought to free itself, but he was strong in his entreaty, and detained it. The Spirit, stronger yet, repulsed him.

Holding up his hands in a last prayer to have his fate reversed, he saw an alteration in the Phantom's hood and dress. It shrunk, collapsed, and dwindled down into a bedpost.

STAVE 5

The End of It

Yes! and the bedpost was his own. The bed was his own, the room was his own. Best and happiest of all, the Time before him was his own, to make amends in!

'I will live in the Past, the Present, and the Future!' Scrooge repeated, as he scrambled out of bed. 'The Spirits of all Three shall strive within me. Oh Jacob Marley! Heaven, and the Christmas Time be praised for this! I say it on my knees, old Jacob, on my knees!'

He was so fluttered and so glowing with his good intentions, that his broken voice would scarcely answer to his call. He had been sobbing violently in his conflict with the Spirit, and his face was wet with tears.

'They are not torn down,' cried Scrooge, folding one of his bed-curtains in his arms, 'they are not torn down, rings and all. They are here: I am here: the shadows of the things that would have been, may be dispelled. They will be. I know they will!'

His hands were busy with his garments all this time: turning them inside out, putting them on upside down, tearing them, mislaying them, making them parties to every kind of extravagance.

'I don't know what to do!' cried Scrooge, laughing and crying in the same breath; and making a perfect Laocoön of himself with his stockings. 'I am as light as a feather, I am as happy as an angel, I am as merry as a school-boy. I am as giddy as a drunken man.

A merry Christmas to everybody! A happy New Year to all the world! Hallo here! Whoop! Hallo!'

He had frisked into the sitting-room, and was now standing there: perfectly winded.

'There's the saucepan that the gruel was in!' cried Scrooge, starting off again, and frisking round the fire-place. 'There's the door, by which the Ghost of Jacob Marley entered! There's the corner where the Ghost of Christmas Present, sat! There's the window where I saw the wandering Spirits! It's all right, it's all true, it all happened. Ha ha ha!'

Really, for a man who had been out of practice for so many years, it was a splendid laugh, a most illustrious laugh. The father of a long, long line of brilliant laughs!

'I don't know what day of the month it is!' said Scrooge. 'I don't know how long I've been among the Spirits. I don't know anything. I'm quite a baby. Never mind. I don't care. I'd rather be a baby. Hallo! Whoop! Hallo here!'

He was checked in his transports by the churches ringing out the lustiest peals he had ever heard. Clash, clang, hammer; ding, dong, bell. Bell, dong, ding; hammer, clang, clash! Oh, glorious, glorious!

Running to the window, he opened it, and put out his head. No fog, no mist; clear, bright, jovial, stirring, cold; cold, piping for the blood to dance to; Golden sunlight; Heavenly sky; sweet fresh air; merry bells. Oh, glorious. Glorious!

'What's to-day?' cried Scrooge, calling downward to a boy in Sunday clothes, who perhaps had loitered in to look about him.

'EH?' returned the boy, with all his might of wonder.

'What's to-day, my fine fellow?' said Scrooge.

'To-day!' replied the boy. 'Why, CHRISTMAS DAY.'

'It's Christmas Day!' said Scrooge to himself. 'I haven't missed it. The Spirits have done it all in one night. They can do anything they like. Of course they can. Of course they can. Hallo, my fine fellow!'

'Hallo!' returned the boy.

'Do you know the Poulterer's, in the next street but one, at the corner?' Scrooge inquired.

'I should hope I did,' replied the lad.

'An intelligent boy!' said Scrooge. 'A remarkable boy! Do you know whether they've sold the prize Turkey that was hanging up there? Not the little prize Turkey: the big one?'

'What, the one as big as me?' returned the boy.

'What a delightful boy!' said Scrooge. 'It's a pleasure to talk to him. Yes, my buck!'

'It's hanging there now,' replied the boy.

'Is it?' said Scrooge. 'Go and buy it'

'Walk-er!' exclaimed the boy.

'No, no,' said Scrooge, 'I am in earnest. Go and buy it, and tell 'em to bring it here, that I may give them the direction where to take it. Come back with the man, and I'll give you a shilling. Come back with him in less than five minutes, and I'll give you half-a-crown!'

The boy was off like a shot. He must have had a steady hand at a trigger who could have got a shot off half so fast.

'I'll send it to Bon Cratchit's!' whispered Scrooge, rubbing his hands, and splitting with a laugh. 'He sha'n't know who sends it. It's twice the size of Tiny Tim. Joe Miller never made such a joke as sending it to Bob's will be!'

The hand in which he wrote the address was not a steady one, but write it he did, somehow, and went down stairs to open the street door, ready for the coming of the poulterer's man. As he stood there, waiting his arrival, the knocker caught his eye.

'I shall love it, as long as I live!' cried Scrooge, patting it with his hand. 'I scarcely ever looked at it before. What an honest expression it has in its face. It's a wonderful knocker! – Here's the Turkey. Hallo! Whoop! How are you? Merry Christmas!'

It *was* a Turkey! He never could have stood upon his legs, that bird. He would have snapped 'em short off in a minute, like sticks of sealing-wax.

'Why, it's impossible to carry that to Camden Town,' said Scrooge. 'You must have a cab.'

The chuckle with which he said this, and the chuckle with which he paid for the Turkey, and the chuckle with which he paid for the cab, and the chuckle with which he recompensed the boy, were only to be exceeded by the chuckle with which he sat down breathless in his chair again, and chuckled till he cried.

Shaving was not an easy task, for his hand continued to shake very much; and shaving requires attention, even when you don't dance while you are at it. But if he had cut the end of his nose off, he would have put a piece of sticking-plaister over it, and been quite satisfied.

He dressed himself 'all in his best,' and at last got out into the streets. The people were by this time pouring forth, as he had seen them with the Ghost of Christmas Present; and walking with his hands behind him, Scrooge regarded every one with a delighted smile. He looked so irresistibly pleasant, in a word, that three or four good-humoured fellows said, 'Good morning, sir! A merry Christmas to you!' And Scrooge said often afterwards, that of all the blithe sounds he had ever heard, those were the blithest in his ears.

He had not gone far, when coming on towards him he beheld the portly gentleman, who had walked into his counting-house the day before, and said, 'Scrooge and Marley's, I believe?' It sent a pang across his heart to think how this old gentleman would look upon him when they met; but he knew what path lay straight before him, and he took it.

'My dear sir,' said Scrooge, quickening his pace, and taking the old gentleman by both his hands. 'How do you do? I hope you succeeded yesterday. It was very kind of you. A merry Christmas to you, sir!'

'Mr. Scrooge?'

'Yes,' said Scrooge. 'That is my name, and I fear it may not be pleasant to you. Allow me to ask your pardon. And will you have the goodness' – here Scrooge whispered in his ear.

'Lord bless me!' cried the gentleman, as if his breath were taken away. 'My dear Mr. Scrooge, are you serious?'

'If you please,' said Scrooge. 'Not a farthing less. A great many back-payments are included in it, I assure you. Will you do me that favour?'

'My dear sir,' said the other, shaking hands with him. 'I don't know what to say to such munifi—'

'Don't say anything, please,' retorted Scrooge. 'Come and see me. Will you come and see me?'

'I will!' cried the old gentleman. And it was clear he meant to do it.

'Thank 'ee,' said Scrooge. 'I am much obliged to you. I thank you fifty times. Bless you!'

He went to church, and walked about the streets, and watched the people hurrying to and fro, and patted children on the head, and questioned beggars, and looked down into the kitchens of houses, and up to the windows, and found that everything could yield him pleasure. He had never dreamed that any walk – that anything – could give him so much happiness. In the afternoon, he turned his steps towards his nephew's house.

He passed the door a dozen times, before he had the courage to go up and knock. But he made a dash, and did it:

'Is your master at home, my dear?' said Scrooge to the girl. Nice girl! Very.

'Yes, sir.'

'Where is he, my love?' said Scrooge.

'He's in the dining-room, sir, along with mistress. I'll show you upstairs, if you please.'

'Thank'ee. He knows me,' said Scrooge, with his hand already on the dining-room lock. 'I'll go in here, my dear.'

He turned it gently, and sidled his face in, round the door. They were looking at the table (which was spread out in great array); for these young housekeepers are always nervous on such points, and like to see that everything is right.

'Fred!' said Scrooge.

Dear heart alive, how his niece by marriage started! Scrooge had forgotten, for the moment, about her sitting in the corner with the footstool, or he wouldn't have done it, on any account.

'Why bless my soul!' cried Fred, 'who's that?'

'It's I. Your uncle Scrooge. I have come to dinner. Will you let me in, Fred?'

Let him in! It is a mercy he didn't shake his arm off. He was at home in five minutes. Nothing could be heartier. His niece looked just the same. So did Topper when *he* came. So did the plump sister when *she* came. So did every one when *they* came. Wonderful party, wonderful games, wonderful unanimity, won-der-ful happiness.

But he was early at the office next morning. Oh, he was early there. If he could only be there first, and catch Bob Cratchit coming late! That was the thing he had set his heart upon.

And he did it; yes, he did! The clock struck nine. No Bob. A quarter past. No Bob. He was full eighteen minutes and a half behind his time. Scrooge sat with his door wide open, that he might see him come into the Tank.

His hat was off, before he opened the door; his comforter too. He was on his stool in a jiffy; driving away with his pen, as if he were trying to overtake nine o'clock.

'Hallo!' growled Scrooge, in his accustomed voice, as near as he could feign it. 'What do you mean by coming here at this time of day?'

'I am very sorry, sir,' said Bob. 'I *am* behind my time.'

'You are?' repeated Scrooge. 'Yes. I think you are. Step this way, sir, if you please.'

'It's only once a year, sir,' pleaded Bob, appearing from the Tank. 'It shall not be repeated. I was making rather merry yesterday, sir.'

'Now, I'll tell you what, my friend,' said Scrooge, 'I am not going to stand this sort of thing any longer. And therefore,' he continued, leaping from his stool, and giving Bob such a dig in the waistcoat that he staggered back into the Tank again; 'and therefore I am about to raise your salary!'

Bob trembled, and got a little nearer to the ruler. He had a momentary idea of knocking Scrooge down with it; holding him; and calling to the people in the court for help and a strait-waistcoat.

'A merry Christmas, Bob!' said Scrooge, with an earnestness that could not be mistaken, as he clapped him on the back. 'A merrier Christmas, Bob, my good fellow, than I have given you for many a year! I'll raise your salary, and endeavour to assist your struggling family, and we will discuss your affairs this very afternoon, over a Christmas bowl of smoking bishop, Bob! Make up the fires, and buy another coal-scuttle before you dot another *i*, Bob Cratchit!'

Scrooge was better than his word. He did it all, and infinitely more; and to Tiny Tim, who did not die, he was a second father. He became as good a friend, as good a master, and as good a man, as the good old city knew, or any other good old city, town, or borough, in the good old world. Some people laughed to see the alteration in him, but he let them laugh, and little heeded them; for he was wise enough to know that nothing ever happened on this globe, for good, at which some people did not have their fill of laughter in the outset; and knowing that such as these would be blind anyway, he thought it quite as well that they should wrinkle up their eyes in grins, as have the malady in less attractive forms. His own heart laughed: and that was quite enough for him.

He had no further intercourse with Spirits, but lived upon the Total Abstinence Principle, ever afterwards; and it was always said of him, that he knew how to keep Christmas well, if any man alive possessed the knowledge. May that be truly said of us, and all of us! And so, as Tiny Tim observed, God Bless Us, Every One!

THE
CHRISTMAS
FEAST

THE CHRISTMAS FEAST

Dickens' conception of Christmas is fundamentally connected to the idea of feasting, embodying as it does the human happiness that he believed the festival should promote. It is a very old idea, nothing to do with the fantasies of rustic gentility and baronial halls beloved of many of his contemporaries. 'Dickens was fighting for that trilogy of eating, drinking and praying which to moderns appears irreverent,' said Chesterton, who knew a thing or two about all three, 'for the holy day which really is a holiday.' It plugs directly into the medieval and the pagan conceptions of a defiance of the evil forces apparently overtaking nature, as well as the notion of storing up strength and food to be able to face the fight ahead. Roderick Marshall describes the Scandinavian festival in the light of the great Nordic sagas: '. . . it was probably Loki who set the great boar's head over the gate of Valhall, and it is more than likely that the ghastly berserkers of the sky fortress, who lived on nothing but boar's flesh and blood, were originally the motley rout of Loki rather than Othin. The wild banqueting in Valhall is, as it were, a perpetual Christmas feast inasmuch as the berserkers are always laying up strength to fight the Frost Giants and have no other function than to prevent their triumph in the midwinter battle.'

For Dickens' poor people, every day was a fight against the forces of poverty, of hardship, of the pessimism which threatened to engulf them. Many of the elements that constitute the Victorians' – and our – Christmas fare have their origins in the old pagan rituals. One which has become a mere decorative notion is the boar's head (wild boar ceased to flourish in Britain in the 13th century). 'It is probable,' says Marshall, 'that the boar's head that presided over the traditional Christmas banquet in many of the northern countries, though most notably perhaps in England – a feast when great supplies of pork were made almost as available to the poor as to the rich, was the representative, at least in pagan times, of the deity who fought and died in giving himself, body and soul, for the heartening of his people in the days of pinching frost and desperation.' Christian and pagan notions intermingle, as with every aspect of Christmas.

For Dickens, it is the coming together of people around a table, the celebration of their humanity, the sharing of their bounty, the reward of indulgence (even if only once a year), that is the essence of the meal, though his ability to render simple comestibles overwhelmingly attractive is astonishing in such an abstemious man.

But behind the sensuality always lies the symbol: the preparation is as life-enhancing as the consumption.

'The party always takes place at uncle George's house,' he writes in *A Christmas Dinner*, 'but grandmamma sends in most of the good things, and grandpapa always will toddle down, all the way to Newgate Market, to buy the turkey, which he engages a porter to bring home behind him in triumph, always insisting on the man's being rewarded with a glass of spirits, over and above his hire, to drink "a merry Christmas" and "a happy new year" to Aunt George. As to grandmamma, she is very secret and mysterious for two or three days beforehand, but not sufficiently so to prevent rumours getting afloat that she has purchased a beautiful new cap with pink

ribbons for each of the servants, together with sundry books, and pen knives, and pencil cases, for the younger branches; to say nothing of divers secret additions to the order originally given by Aunt George at the pastry cook's, such as another dozen of mince pies for the dinner, and a large plum cake for the children. On Christmas Eve, grandmamma is always in excellent spirits, and after employing all the children, during the day, in stoning the plums, and all that, insists, regularly every year, on uncle George coming down into the kitchen, taking off his coat, and stirring the pudding for half an hour or so, which uncle George good-humouredly does, to the vociferous delight of the children and servants.'

The valiant struggle of the Cratchits to make their meagre ingredients feel like a feast is triumphantly successful, and one of the most affecting sections of *A Christmas Carol*.

There never was such a goose. Bob said he didn't believe there ever was such a goose cooked. Its tenderness and flavour, size and cheapness, were the themes of universal admiration. Eked out by the apple-sauce and mashed potatoes, it was a sufficient dinner for the whole family; indeed, as Mrs. Cratchit said with great delight (surveying one small atom of a bone upon the dish), they hadn't ate it all at last! Yet everyone had had enough, and the youngest Cratchits in particular, were steeped in sage and onion to the eyebrows! But now, the plates being changed by Miss Belinda, Mrs. Cratchit left the room alone – too nervous to bear witnesses – to take the pudding up, and bring it in.

Suppose it should not be done enough! Suppose it should break in turning out! Suppose somebody should have got over the wall of the back-yard, and stolen it, while they were merry with the goose: a supposition at which the two young Cratchits became livid! All sorts of horrors were supposed.

Bob and Martha Cratchit have somehow ensured that with the derisory emolument he has squeezed out of Scrooge, they have on their table – in reduced form, but still – what every family in England expects to have on its table on a Christmas Day.

LEFT: Christmas Day, *painting by George Hardie, 1867*

The goose had been established as Christmas fare since the time of Elizabeth I, although it was a luxury, only affordable to a poor man if he belonged to a Goose Club, paying in so much a week, and of course, being cheated along the way. The Temperance League waged a war against the Goose Clubs, which were often equivalent to pubs, and which lured its members into spending their nugatory salaries on the demon drink.

> Tom Bates was once a workman good: in sad and evil hour
> He joined the 'Goose' Club, and, alas! was soon in Fillpot's power.
> In Fillpot's house he spends his all, and runs awhile in debt,
> For he that will a drunkard be must soon in trouble get.
>
> Unhappy Bates! at evening hour he hears the tap-room brawl,
> And, mingling with the company, he slinks behind them all.
> But wary Fillpot finds him out; looks at his unpaid score;
> Secures his hat and ragged coat, and kicks him from his door.
>
> And thus that fox, the publican, who plays at fast and loose,
> Devours the flesh and picks the bones of his deluded goose.
> My tale is told – I seek to give offence to none alive;
> But Goose Clubs do more harm than good, and ought not to survive.

The goose thus purchased would be cooked, like the Cratchits', at the bakers'; few working-class households had ovens, so the baker, for a small consideration, would leave his alight on Christmas Day. This is where Dickens tells us the younger Cratchits go to fetch the goose. Thanks to the influx of poultry from France and Germany in the 1840s, a goose was much more readily available than formerly. Turkey too had a long tradition of Christmas consumption – at least since the 16th century when it was introduced to Europe by the conquistadors on their way back from America – and was being reared in ever greater quantities, mostly in Norfolk, Suffolk and Cambridge. Getting the creatures to the metropolis was a considerable task. They had to walk, their feet shod or wrapped in rags or coated with tar; the journey down could take weeks. Later, they were slaughtered on the farms and conveyed by coach, a three-day journey; it was only with the development of the railways that they finally became accessible to the general population. The poulterers stayed open on Christmas Day, which is how Scrooge was able to order one in the exuberance of his new conversion. In some households – not the Cratchits', alas – the bird was triumphantly surmounted by an Alderman's Chain, a string of sausages served up in a string.

The Christmas pudding that was such a feature of the Cratchits' Christmas was on every menu, and the making of it was a central event of the holiday period.

In a household where there are five or six children, the eldest not above ten or eleven, the making of the pudding is indeed an event, reported the *Illustrated London News* in 1848.

It is thought of days, if not weeks, before. To be allowed to share in the noble work, is a prize for young ambition ... Lo! the lid is raised, curiosity stands on tip toe, eyes sparkle with anticipation, little hands are clapped in ecstasy, almost too great to find expression in words. The hour arrives – the moment wished and feared – wished, oh! How intensely; feared, not in the event, but lest envious fate should not allow it to be an event, and mar the glorious Concoction in its very birth. And then when it is dished, when all fears of this kind are over, when the roast beef has been removed, when the pudding, in all the glory of its own splendour, shines upon the table,

ABOVE: *Taking home the Christmas dinner cooked in the baker's oven, 1840s*

how eager is the anticipation of the near delight! How beautifully it steams! How delicious it smells! How round it is! A kiss is round, the horizon is round, the earth is round, the moon is round, the sun and stars, and all the host of heaven are round. So is plum pudding.

The same paper regarded British prowess in this area as a matter of patriotic pride: 'The French have no idea how to make a plum pudding, but some friendly genius instructed the English in the art ... the plum pudding symbolises so much English antiquity – English superstition – English enterprise – English generosity – and above all, English taste.'

It was generally regarded as something of a marvel. The Cratchits', prepared in their copper washing tub, is accompanied by a great wave of excitement.

Hallo! A great deal of steam! The pudding was out of the copper. A smell like a washing-day! That was the cloth. A smell like an eating-house and a pastry cook's next door to each other, with a laundress's next door to that! That was the pudding! In half a minute Mrs. Cratchit entered: flushed, but smiling proudly: with the pudding, like a speckled cannon-ball, so hard and firm, blazing in half of half-a-quartern of ignited brandy, and bedight with Christmas holly stuck into the top.

Oh, a wonderful pudding, Bob Cratchit said, and calmly too, that he regarded it as the greatest success achieved by Mrs. Cratchit since their marriage. Mrs. Cratchit said that now the weight was off her mind, she would confess she had had her doubts about the quantity of flour. Everybody had

ABOVE: *Making a Christmas pudding, 19th-century Christmas card*

something to say about it, but nobody said or thought it was at all a small pudding for a large family. It would have been flat heresy to do so. Any Cratchit would have blushed to hint at such a thing.

In Boz's early sketch describing a Christmas dinner, there is a similar level of excitement:

When, at last, a stout servant staggers in with a gigantic pudding, with a sprig of holly in the top, there is such a laughing, and shouting, and clapping of little chubby hands, and kicking up of fat dumpy legs, as can only be equalled by the applause with which the astonishing feat of pouring lighted brandy into mince pies is received by the younger visitors. Then the dessert! and the wine!

Like mince pies, which were originally made with shredded meat, the plum pudding had once contained boiled beef and mutton, and was in fact a form of frumenty, containing in addition raisins, currants, prunes, wines, spices. It became plum pudding – 'plum' because of the prunes which were used in its making before the arrival of raisins – when it was thickened with eggs, breadcrumbs, dried fruit, ale, and spirits. The Puritans of course banned it – far too many enjoyable ingredients – and it was not officially restored to circulation until the reign of George I. The medieval Church, as usual assiduously seeking to attach itself to the popularity of Christmas, decreed that puddings should be made on the 25th Sunday after Trinity,

ABOVE: Pudding Time, *from* Illustrations of Time, *1827*

and prepared with thirteen ingredients – to represent Christ and the twelve apostles: the pudding was to be stirred by every member of the family in turn from east to west, in honour of the Magi and their supposed journey in that direction.

Mince pies seem to have had their origin in a representation of Christ's manger; they were oblong, and inside was a pastry baby. According to tradition, if one ate a mince pie on each of the twelve days of Christmas, one would have twelve days of happiness, which was, in a sense, what the whole feast was about: enjoying oneself so much that the memory of it would last the long year until it returned.

Mulled wine offered immediate gratification. The Cratchits' is, like everything else at their feast, cheaply made:

> Bob, turning up his cuffs – as if, poor fellow, they were capable of being made more shabby – compounded some hot mixture in a jug with gin and lemons, and stirred it round and round and put it on the hob to simmer.

But it is sufficient to its purpose.

> At last the dinner was all done, the cloth was cleared, the hearth swept, and the fire made up. The compound in the jug being tasted and considered perfect, apples and oranges were put upon the table, and a shovel-full of chestnuts on the fire. Then all the Cratchit family drew round the hearth, in what Bob Cratchit called a circle, meaning half a one; and at Bob Cratchit's elbow stood the family display of glass; two tumblers, and a custard-cup without a handle.
>
> These held the hot stuff from the jug, however, as well as golden goblets would have done; and Bob served it out with beaming looks, while the chestnuts on the fire sputtered and crackled noisily. Then Bob proposed:
>
> 'A Merry Christmas to us all, my dears. God bless us!'

When Scrooge in his reformed state at the end of the novel wants to sit and talk to Bob about his plans for Bob's future, he does so over a Smoking Bishop, which is made by pouring red wine (so much more expensive than the gin which Bob uses) over bitter oranges and mulled in a vessel with a long funnel, after which sugar and spices are added. The purple hue resulting from this process gives it its Episcopal association.

Dickens had great faith in the humanizing power of the Christmas feast. He was thinking, as always, principally of the poor, and in his next Christmas book he positively attacks the rich, not so much for their wealth as for their indifference to the suffering of others. But the idea of marking Christmas with repleteness runs through his writings. Despite David Copperfield's dismal Christmas dinner with a cowed Joe Gargery and an implacable Mrs Joe, and notwithstanding his having set the murder in *Edwin Drood* on Christmas Day, he often returns to the Christmas feast, joyous and celebratory even when spent alone. At the climax of *Dr Marigold*, the story he read on his reading tours to such powerful sentimental effect, the title character, a travelling salesman, settles into his cart for Christmas:

I had had a first-rate autumn of it, and on the twenty-third of December, one thousand eight hundred and sixty-four, I found myself at Uxbridge, Middlesex, clean sold out. So I jogged up to London with the old horse, light and easy, to have my Christmas-Eve and Christmas-Day alone by the fire in the Library Cart, and then to buy a regular new stock of goods all round, to sell 'em again and get the money. I am a neat hand at cookery, and I'll tell you what I knocked up for my Christmas-Eve dinner in the Library Cart. I knocked up a beefsteak pudding for one, with two kidneys, a dozen oysters, and a couple of mushrooms, thrown in. It's a pudding to put a man in good humour with everything, except the two bottom buttons of his waistcoat.

It is a serene vignette of the warming power of the Christmas feast, perfectly setting the scene for the touching resolution which follows it. 'Dickens' theory of life was entirely wrong,' Thomas Carlyle said of the friend for whose political and intellectual views he had little time, though he acknowledged his genius as a creative artist. 'He believed that men should be buttered up, and the world made soft and accommodating for them, and all sorts of fellows should have turkey for Christmas dinner.' Exactly.

ABOVE: Scrooge and Bob Cratchit, *by John Leech*

NEW TRADITIONS,
OLD TRADITIONS

———◦◦◦———

New Traditions, Old Traditions

Dickens' contribution to redefining Christmas was a very particular one, as we have seen, but his activity in the field was matched by a huge effort of invention and reinvention on the part of his fellow Victorians, whose energy in these matters is constantly astonishing, and whose complexity of motives is remarkable. Dickens himself had little to do with the increasing popularity of the associated aspects of Christmas, but he was fully aware of most of them. Of the contemporary revival of wassailing – in the sense of carol-singing – for example, we read little in Dickens' books, but the wassail bowl itself is much to the fore, a symbol of good cheer and shared pleasures, a bowl filled with good things, from which everyone's drink is dispensed. He himself loved to prepare the punchbowl, and – as with most things he did – he was very good at it, though, also characteristically, he somehow managed to avoid actually drinking from it himself.

In fact the word 'wassail', Saxon in origin, has neither an alcoholic nor a musical association. It is a salutation, pure and simple: *Wachs Heil*, meaning 'be of good health'; in Old English this became *Wes Hel*. The association with Christmas is somewhat obscure, but by the Elizabethan period it was well established that throughout the festive season, singers (already known as wassailers) would sing a few verses of their song on the porch of a house and then be invited inside, where they would finish their rendition. Then alms would be given; if not, ill fortune would descend on the hosts. For the wassailers' part, they had to drink from the host's wassail bowl; there is no recorded history of any reluctance to do so. Sometimes, the singers would take round a wassail bowl of their own which they would drain on the doorstep in the expectation that the householder they were serenading would replenish it.

In addition to such sociable traditions, with their clear origins in pagan customs – the intemperate drinking, the sense of the division between the warm welcoming interior and the dark, frightening exterior – we find customs which reveal an animistic relationship

PAGES 124–5: Christmas Time: The Blodgett Family, *1864, painting by Eastman Johnson (1824–1906)*
LEFT: A Carol for a Wassail Bowl, *1840s*

to nature. In Herefordshire animals were wassailed, punch and ale being poured over them; and there is widespread evidence of the striking tradition of wassailing trees surviving until very recently. At Twelfth Night, villagers would surround a tree at dusk and shoot bullets through the branches, banging pots and pans, making a raucous din to scare off evil spirits. Then the tree would be splashed with wassail, which was also poured around its roots. After this, the participants bowed to the tree and sang the wassail song to ensure a good crop.

Now, none of this is what interested the Victorians in wassailing, nor, it must be admitted, Dickens himself. 'If some Radical contemporary and friend of Dickens,' Chesterton wrote, 'had happened to say to him that in defending the mince-pies and the mummeries of Christmas he was defending a piece of barbaric and brutal ritualism, doomed to disappear in the light of reason along with the Boy-Bishop and the Lord of Misrule, I am not sure that Dickens (though he was one of the readiest and most rapid masters of reply in history) would have found it very easy upon his own principles to answer.' Wassailing, for both Dickens and his contemporaries, was something worth reviving because it created a continuity with a past which seemed rapidly to be disappearing, and because it was a symbol of inclusiveness.

Carol-singing fell somewhat into the same category. For over a hundred years, antiquarians had been lamenting the death of the carol, and by extension the whole oral tradition. With some urgency Davies Gilbert, the great collector of folk songs, had exhorted his readers 'in every part of England' to collect 'every carol that may be singing at Christmas time in the year 1825, and convey these carols to him at their earliest convenience, with accounts of manners and customs peculiar to the people'. Carols were perceived as coming for the most part from Cornwall, from the Midlands and from the north, though in reality they seem to have been spread fairly widely across the country. Modern carols were despised as corrupt and of inferior standard – 'the veriest trash imaginable', thought Miss Butt, in 1839, compared to the good old traditional songs; as an example of what a proper carol should be, Washington Irving quotes a bilingual medieval one in *The Sketchbook of Geoffrey Crayon*:

Caput apri defero
Reddens laudi Domino.
The boar's head in hand bring I,
With garlands gay and rosemary.
I pray you all singe merily
Qui estis in convivio.

In fact, the carol as a form had a far from pious origin, being French and usually rather filthy; the Church, as always seeking to tame popular tradition while exploiting the affection in which it was held, had claimed carols for Jesus, to the point where they had become 'an oasis of genuine, affectionate religion', the only sort for which Dickens, of course, had any time. The new urban proletariat, bewildered and deracinated, trying to live as if they

were still in the country, tenaciously clung to their carols. The middle classes encouraged the tradition, eagerly seizing upon any point of contact between religion and the poor; these new working-class people seemed to them to be dangerously lacking in both spirituality and morality. The spiritual bankruptcy of the Anglican dispensation was widely acknowledged, providing a fertile soil in which Methodism could flourish, and Methodism's progress was inextricably intertwined with music, above all the choral tradition. Singing in choirs brought people together in an analogue of the communal relationship itself, blending together rhythmically, harmonically and tunefully; carols were a fine medium for this, as the neo-Catholic Oxford Movement, with its revival of medieval piety, also found.

Dickens chose the Christmas carol as the embodiment of the sort of song he wanted to sing in his little Christmas novel, the one which would deliver the 'sledge-hammer blow' he felt was so urgently needed. In the third stave of that book, an old miner sings a carol; and in *The Pickwick Papers*, Dickens (not otherwise noted for his verse) actually created one for Mr Wardle to sing:

Thus saying, the merry old gentleman, in a good, round, sturdy voice, commenced without more ado –

ABOVE: *A ballad-monger and his family singing and selling Christmas carols, 1847*

A Christmas Carol

I care not for Spring; on his fickle wing
Let the blossoms and buds be borne;
He woos them amain with his treacherous rain,
And he scatters them ere the morn.
An inconstant elf, he knows not himself,
Nor his own changing mind an hour,
He'll smile in your face, and, with witty grimace,
He'll wither your youngest flower.

A mild harvest night, by the tranquil light
Of the modest and gentle moon,
Has a far sweeter sheen for me, I ween,
Than the broad and unblushing noon.
But every leaf awakens my grief,
As it lieth beneath the tree;
So let Autumn air be never so fair,
It by no means agrees with me.

Let the Summer sun to his bright home run,
He shall never be sought by me;
When he's dimmed by a cloud I can laugh aloud
And care not how sulky he be!
For his darling child is the madness wild
That sports in fierce fever's train;
And when love is too strong, it don't last long,
As many have found to their pain.

But my song I troll out, for CHRISTMAS Stout,
The hearty, the true, and the bold;
A bumper I drain, and with might and main
Give three cheers for this Christmas old!
We'll usher him in with a merry din
That shall gladden his joyous heart,
And we'll keep him up, while there's bite or sup,
And in fellowship good, we'll part.

In his fine honest pride, he scorns to hide
One jot of his hard-weather scars;
They're no disgrace, for there's much the same trace
On the cheeks of our bravest tars.
Then again I sing till the roof doth ring
And it echoes from wall to wall –
To the stout old wight, fair welcome to-night,
As the King of the Seasons all!

This entirely secular carol, while doing little, perhaps, for Dickens' reputation as a poet, is fully informed with the vigour and generosity of his feeling for the season. In a piece published in *All the Year Round*, he speaks more intensely of the same thing: '. . . the images once associated with the sweet old Waits, the softened music in the night, ever unalterable! Encircled by the social thoughts of Christmas time, still let the

benignant figure of my childhood stand unchanged! In every cheerful image and suggestion that the season brings, may the bright star that rested above the poor roof, be the star of all the Christian world.' Interestingly, in Percy Dearmer's *A Carol Play of 1926*, quoted by Weightman, the revival of carols and the revival of Christmas are strongly linked, and both are inextricably bound up with Dickens himself. 'I am come to wish you a merry Christmas,' Dearmer's Prologue says. 'A hundred years ago, Englishmen had almost forgotten about the Christmas spirit. They thought only of being respectable and making as much money as they possibly could; and the poor were oppressed and their old Christmas ways of beauty and goodwill were despised and forgotten. There arose a great man, Charles Dickens, who grew up in poverty and neglect, and who loved the good heart of the poor, and he made all men understand that to be jolly and generous is to be Christian. Then I came back to England again, and the carols came back with me: a few poor Waits had remembered them during the long years when the clever and fashionable and the powerful had forgotten.'

The games associated with Christmas – a peculiarly English phenomenon – are of course endlessly celebrated by Dickens, from the Blind Man's Buff at which Topper so disgracefully cheats at Scrooge's nephew's party, to the Snapdragon vigorously pursued by the young in *A Christmas Dinner*, to the mistletoe-kissing at Dingley Dell. These games have their roots, needless to say, in the Saturnalia, and found their definitive form in the Middle Ages; many of them have an element of the forbidden about them, stolen kisses

ABOVE: *Blind Man's Buff, 1849*

being a central element in more than one. For the Victorians with their new moral rectitude, this was a particularly sought-after release. In medieval England, the games had an equally practical purpose: relieving the bloated sensations resultant from uncommonly high levels of consumption. Christmas really did come but once a year, and for many it was the best meal they had, during which they did not stint themselves. (The humorist Frank Muir in his droll Christmas compendium reports a Norman in-between-courses tradition: 'they actually made a thing of this shaking-down process. Everyone would stand up, hold hands, and dance round and round the table singing *En Sacant, En Sacant!* a literal translation of which might be, "Put it in the sack! Put it in the sack!"')

If good eating was a rare phenomenon, to be relished to the hilt, then so were games. During the reign of Henry VIII, the working class was prohibited from playing them at any other time, on penalty of a crippling fine:

> Tables, Tennis, Dice, Cards, Bowls, Clash, Coyting, Logating or any other unlawful Game, out of Christmas, under pain of 20 shillings to be forfeit every time; and in Christmas time to play at any of the said games in their Master's House, or in their Master's presence.

As usual with such draconian laws, the proclamation was no doubt honoured more in the breach than the observance, but its existence perhaps infused the games in question with a particular energy and abandon.

By the time of the Puritan Commonwealth, of course, the ban was total and fiercely enforced. Many games died; but Snapdragon survived triumphantly, a special favourite of the Victorians. It was a test of skill and intrepidity: in a darkened room, a dish

ABOVE: Capering, *from 'A Search after the Comfortable'. A first idea for* The Pickwick Papers, *drawing by Robert Seymour (1800–36)*

of dried fruits doused in brandy was set alight and floated in a bowl of water. The game was to snatch the fruit out of the jaws of the flame and consume it.

> Here he comes with flaming bowl,
> Don't be mean to take his toll,
> Snip! Snap! Dragon!
>
> Take care you don't take too much,
> Be not greedy in your clutch,
> Snip! Snap! Dragon!
>
> With his blue and lapping tongue
> Many of you will be stung,
> Snip! Snap! Dragon!
>
> For he snaps at all that comes
> Snatching at his feast of plums,
> Snip! Snap! Dragon!
>
> But Old Christmas makes him come,
> Though he looks so fee' fa' fum'
> Snip! Snap! Dragon!
>
> Don't 'ee fear him, be but bold
> But he gaan, his flamou are cold
> Snip! Snap! Dragon!

The sexual content of Snapdragon is as low as that of mistletoe-kissing was high. *Viscum album* is, by technical definition, a shrubby parasite, which certainly puts it in its place. In Druidic ritual, however, it was deemed to be the healer of all things, its relation to

ABOVE: Gaming, *from 'A Search after the Comfortable'*

the host tree lending it a mystical significance; its capacity to grow on oak throughout the winter suggested to the ancient Britons that it contained the life force of the tree itself. After a sacrificial rite, sprigs of mistletoe would be taken home and placed over the door as protection against thunder, lightning and evil spirits and as a fertility talisman – from which originated the kissing tradition, unique to the British Isles. Right up to Edwardian times, the rule was that after each kiss, a berry was plucked off; when there were no more berries, the kissing had to stop.

Pick a berry off the mistletoe
For ev'ry kiss that's given.
When the berries have all gone,
There's an end to kissing.

Sam Weller takes full advantage of the tradition at Wardle's party; and even Pickwick, otherwise a stranger to osculatory activity, lends himself to a little seasonal gallantry with old Mrs Wardle. This increase in tactility in a race whose sensual aloofness was growing apace was, of course, entirely approved of by Dickens, who was as indifferent to the Druidic origins of the practice as he was to the Christian extrapolations which maintained that mistletoe had once been a full-sized tree out of which Christ's cross was fashioned, shrinking to its current depleted size from shame, and thereafter banned from churches. For Dickens it was simply one of many decorations which helped to create the festive, carnival atmosphere which was the glory and the point of the season.

As far as Christmas cards go, Dickens seems to have no connection whatever with them (although his daughter Kate Perugini Dickens designed some after his death). The idea

ABOVE: *Plate showing Christmas Eve at Mr Wardle's, from* The Pickwick Papers. *From an original drawing by 'Phiz' (Hablot Knight Browne) (1815–82)*

of the Dickens Christmas, of course, provided the classic imagery for many of them. In fact the very first recorded Christmas card, designed by J.C. Horsley for Henry Cole (later to be the first Director of the Victoria and Albert Museum) appeared in Christmas 1843, exactly when *A Christmas Carol* made its first appearance, and its theme was identical to that of Dickens' novella: it was in the form of a triptych, the central panel of which showed several generations of a family holding up their glasses and toasting the viewer, while the side panels carry scenes of the poor being fed and clothed. At a shilling a time, it was rather expensive; the following year, W.C.T. Dobson produced a somewhat cheaper card, 'The Spirit of Christmas', which sold over a thousand more copies than Horsley's had. In commissioning that first card, Cole had been inspired by the 'Christmas pieces' which in the previous century school-

masters had set their pupils to work on: end-of-year samplers of writing exercises with engraved borders to show how well the students had done. These became more elaborate and more colourful; by the 1820s, their borders were enhanced by colour. All the elements were there, waiting for someone to unify it into something more flamboyant and more commercial.

Once the tradition was established, manufacturers began to adorn cards with silk, satin, plush and brocade. After the initial, properly Dickensian beginning, there seemed to be a certain amount of confusion as to the appropriate imagery – some showed naughty nymphs, while German cards tended to depict murders and spanking scenes. In the 1870s, cheap printing arrived and the custom of sending Christmas cards became universal; the imagery settled largely on representations of snowy rustic scenes, another motif

ABOVE: Mrs Perugini *(Dickens' second daughter, Kate), 1880, painting by Sir John Everett Millais (1829–96)*

ABOVE: A Merry Christmas and a happy new year to ye, *Christmas card engraved by G. Hunt* (fl. 1833)

ABOVE: *Facsimile reproduction of the first Christmas card, designed by J.C. Horsley for Henry Cole, 1843*
BELOW: The Same to You, Sir, & Many of 'Em; A Merry Christmas & a Happy New Year in London, *Christmas card engraved by G. Hunt, 1827*

of nostalgia. Christmases in the 1830s and 1840s had been notable for their harshness; thereafter, white Christmases were the exception, one more example of the Victorian aptitude for creating instant myths.

Christmas crackers were another Victorian innovation: the confectioner Tom Smith, who wanted to spruce up his bon-bons, had the happy idea of causing them to explode when they were pulled apart. Thinking of the sharp-shooting Russian tribal warriors who haunted the Victorian imagination (particularly after the Crimean War in 1853–6) he called them 'cosaques'. They were rather substantial at the beginning; Smith commissioned well-known artists to design them, and famous authors to write the mottoes. The presents were substantial, too: fans, jewellery, head-dresses; there were special crackers for specific groups, those for spinsters dauntingly containing a wedding ring, a night cap, and a bottle of hair dye. Weightman wickedly remarks that the cracker was 'tailor-made for the Victorian family Christmas dinner – a feeble spark which perfectly suited the demure

ABOVE: *Fores's Christmas Envelope, published by Messrs Fores, c.1840*

sensibilities of the class, and mimicked the more ancient communal fire festivals which were rapidly disappearing from the scene: once paper hats were added, it became a perfect little package of pagan ritual for the family table: firs and funny hats without the Saturnalian excess.'

The Christmas novelty to which Dickens responded most warmly was the Christmas tree, at the beginning of the 19th century widely and correctly called 'the German Christmas tree'. These trees were traditional only in certain parts of Germany: in 1605 they seemed to be quite a new thing in Strasbourg: 'thereon hang roses cut out of many-coloured paper, apples, wafers, gold-foil, sweets, etc. . . .' There is a fine description of the phenomenon in E.T.A. Hoffmann's *The Nutcracker* of 1816:

The great Christmas Tree on the table bore many apples of silver and of gold, and all of its branches were heavy with bud and blossom, consisting of sugar almonds, many-tinted bon-bons, and all sorts of things to eat. Perhaps the prettiest thing about this wonder-tree, however, was the fact that in all the recesses of its spreading branches hundreds of little tapers descended like stars, inviting the children to pluck its flowers and fruit. Also, all around the tree on every side everything shone and glittered in the loveliest manner. Oh, how many beautiful things . . .

The British Hanoverian monarchs George III and William IV had Christmas trees; German merchants living in Manchester introduced them to that city in the 1830s. But the 1845 Christmas edition of the *Illustrated London News* felt that it needed to describe to its readers the significance of German Christmas trees, or 'Trees of Love', offering advice on how to exhibit the tree, suggesting that fruit and flowers and small presents

ABOVE: The First Christmas Tree in Ried, Germany, *1848, painting by Franz Ignaz Pollinger*

were appropriate hangings; the danger of fire from the candles pegged to the branches was helpfully pointed out.

The turning point in the history of the Christmas tree was its adoption by the young Queen Victoria and her German consort Prince Albert; a famous picture, again in the *Illustrated London News*, of the Royal Family Christmas at Windsor in 1848, with the present-bedecked tree in the foreground, ensured that every family felt that they must have one. Royal endorsement meant a great deal in 1848.

***

In the 1852 edition of *All the Year Round* Dickens composed a reverie about a Christmas tree; the piece vividly evokes Victorian middle-class Christmas:

> I have been looking on, this evening, at a merry company of children assembled round that pretty German toy, a Christmas Tree! The tree was planted in the middle of a great round table, and towered high above their heads. It was brilliantly lighted by a multitude of little tapers; and everywhere sparkled and glittered with bright objects. There were rosy-cheeked dolls, hiding behind the green leaves; there were real watches (with movable hands, at least, and an endless capacity of being wound up) dangling from innumerable twigs; there were French-polished tables, chairs, bedsteads, wardrobes, eight-day clocks, and various other articles of domestic furniture (wonderfully made, in tin, at Wolverhampton), perched among the boughs, as if in preparation for some fairy housekeeping; there were jolly, broad-faced little men, much more agreeable in appearance than many real men – and no wonder, for their heads took off, and showed them to be full of sugar-plums; there were fiddles and drums; there were tambourines, books, work-boxes, paint-boxes, sweetmeat-boxes, peep-show boxes, all kinds of boxes; there were trinkets for the elder girls, far brighter than any grown-up gold and jewels; there were baskets and pincushions in all devices; there were gems, swords, and banners; there were witches standing in enchanted rings of pasteboard, to tell fortunes; there were teetotums, humming-tops, needle-cases, pen-wipers, smelling-bottles, conversation-cards, bouquet-holders; real fruit, made artificially dazzling with gold leaf; imitation apples, pears, and walnuts, crammed with surprises; in short, as a pretty child, before me, delightedly whispered to another pretty child, her bosom friend, 'There was everything, and more.' This motley collection

RIGHT: *The Royal Family around the Christmas tree at Windsor Castle, 1848, engraving after J.L. Williams (c.1815–77)*

of odd objects, clustering on the tree like magic fruit, and flashing back the bright looks directed towards it from every side – some of the diamond-eyes admiring it were hardly on a level with the table, and a few were languishing in timid wonder on the bosoms of pretty mothers, aunts, and nurses – made a lively realisation of the fancies of childhood; and set me thinking how all the trees that grow and all the things that come into existence on the earth, have their wild adornments at that well-remembered time.

Dickens then begins to develop the autobiographical aspect of his relationship to the tree, and his childish discovery of the world:

Being now at home again, and alone, the only person in the house awake, my thoughts are drawn back, by a fascination which I do not care to resist, to my own childhood. I begin to consider, what do we all remember best upon the branches of the Christmas Tree of our own young Christmas days, by which we climbed to real life. Straight, in the middle of the room, cramped in the freedom of its growth by no encircling walls or soon-reached ceiling, a shadowy tree arises; and, looking up into the dreamy brightness of its top – for I observe, in this tree, the singular property that it appears to grow downward towards the earth – I look into my youngest Christmas recollections! – All toys at first, I find. Up yonder, among the green holly and red berries, is the Tumbler with his hands in his pockets, who wouldn't lie down, but whenever he was put upon the floor, persisted in rolling his fat body about, until he rolled himself still, and brought those lobster eyes of his to bear upon me when I affected to laugh very much, in my heart of hearts was extremely doubtful of him. Close beside him is that infernal snuff-box, out of which there sprang a demoniacal Counsellor in a black gown, with an obnoxious head of hair, and a red cloth mouth, wide open, who was not to be endured on any terms, but could not be put away either; for he used suddenly, in a highly magnified state, to fly out of Mammoth Snuff-boxes in dreams, when least expected. Nor is the frog with cobbler's wax on his tail, far off; for there was no knowing where he wouldn't jump; and when he flew over the candle, and came upon one's hand with that spotted back – red on a green ground – he was horrible. The cardboard lady in a blue-silk skirt, who was stood up against the candlestick to dance, and whom I see on the same branch, was milder, and was beautiful; but I can't say as much for the larger cardboard man, who used to be hung against the wall and pulled by a string; there was a sinister expression in that nose of his; and when he got his legs round his neck (which he very often did), he was ghastly, and not a creature to be alone with. When did that dreadful Mask first look at me? Who put it on, and why was I so frightened that the sight of it is an era in my life? It is not a hideous visage in itself; it is even meant to be droll;

why then were its stolid features so intolerable? Surely not because it hid the wearer's face. An apron would have done as much; and though I should have preferred even the apron away, it would not have been absolutely insupportable, like the mask.

He continues to elaborate the child's experience with typical regard for its darkness as well as its lights.

Was it the immovability of the mask? The doll's face was immovable, but I was not afraid of her. Perhaps that fixed and set change coming over a real face, infused into my quickened heart some remote suggestion and dread of the universal change that is to come on every face, and make it still? Nothing reconciled me to it. No drummers, from whom proceeded a melancholy chirping on the turning of a handle; no regiment of soldiers, with a mute band, taken out of a box, and fitted, one by one, upon a stiff and lazy little set of lazy-tongs; no old woman, made of wires and a brown-paper composition, cutting up a pie for two small children; could give me permanent comfort, for a long time. Nor was it any satisfaction to be shown the mask, and see that it was made of paper, or to have it locked up and be assured that no one wore it. The mere recollection of that fixed face, the mere knowledge of its existence anywhere, was sufficient to awake me in the night all perspiration and horror, with 'O I know it's coming! O the mask!'

Finally he recalls the central core of his dream of Christmas, the memory of the beloved departed, and the thought of those absent from the feast.

A moment's pause, O vanishing tree, of which the lower boughs are dark to me as yet, and let me look once more! I know there are blank spaces on thy branches, where eyes that I have loved, have shone and smiled; from which they are departed. But, far above, I see the raiser of the dead girl, and the Widow's Son; and God is good! If Age be hiding for me in the unseen portion of thy downward growth, O may I, with a grey head, turn a child's heart to that figure yet, and a child's trustfulness and confidence! – Now, the tree is decorated with bright merriment, and song, and dance, and cheerfulness. And they are welcome. Innocent and welcome be they ever held, beneath the branches of the Christmas Tree, which cast no gloomy shadow! But, as it sinks into the ground, I hear a whisper going through the leaves. 'This, in commemoration of the law of love and kindness, mercy and compassion. This, in remembrance of Me!'

BEYOND DICKENS' CHRISTMAS

BEYOND DICKENS' CHRISTMAS

Like so much else in the 21st century, Christmas as we know it is essentially the same everywhere in the world because of America's influence. By the end of the 19th century, American economic power had grown so rapidly that Henry Luce could claim without undue hubris that the following hundred years constituted the American Century. The genesis of the modern Christmas, as Goldy and Purdue observe, 'draws selectively upon a host of European traditions but was nevertheless forged by Anglo-American cultural influences in the early and mid-19th century'. Dickens is overpoweringly the most important figure in its development, but the interpenetration of elements in the process is subtle and complex.

It has sometimes been claimed that Dickens lifted his conception of Christmas wholesale from Washington Irving. As we have seen, that is scarcely tenable: the American writer's influence is undoubtedly present, but even in *The Pickwick Papers* the carnival spirit that moves Dickens' vision, all vigour and earthy exuberance, is profoundly different to the dreamy, ritualized world depicted in the antiquarian sketches of 'Geoffrey Crayon', a sort of soft-focus medieval fancy-dress party; even the food dresses up. Irving felt obliged to defend the authenticity of his account of British Christmas observances and in December 1831 he took the new American Ambassador, Mark le Brun, to the homes of various friends, in each of which could be found some of the customs and traditions he had merged into his glowing tableau of the proceedings genially supervised by the – admittedly imaginary – Squire of Bracebridge Hall.

It is equally clear, however, that Irving drew not only the spirit of his Christmas but also many of its details from the work of Sir Walter Scott, whose would-be ancestral home, Abbotsford, he had visited while Scott was in the throes of writing *Rob Roy*. It is Scott's yearning for a world where knights were bold and damsels fair, the board groaning and the retainers faithful which underpins Irving's vision.

PAGES 144–5: *Caricature of Charles Dickens, title page illustration from* L'Eclipse *magazine, 14 June 1848, coloured lithograph after a drawing by André Gill (Louis Alexandre Gosset de Guines) (1840–85)*
RIGHT: *Christmas dinner in the baronial hall, engraving from Washington Irving's* Old Christmas

And well our Sires of old
Loved when the year its course had rolled
And brought blithe Christmas back again
With all his hospitable train . . .
Then open'd wide the Baron's hall
To vassal, tenant, serf, and all . . .
The wassel round, in good brown bowls,
Garnish'd with ribbons, blithely trowls.
There the huge sirloin reek'd; hard by
Plum-porridge stood, and Christmas pie . . .
England was merry England when
Old Christmas brought his sports again.
'Twas Christmas broached the mightiest ale;
'Twas Christmas told the merriest tale;
A Christmas gambol oft could cheer
The poor man's heart through half the year.

To cite this passage is not to accuse Irving of plagiarism, but to underline again that the widely reported death of Christmas was greatly exaggerated. Both Dickens and Irving in their different ways tapped into a tradition – and a set of symbols – which was deeply established.

In 1820, when Irving was writing, America needed Christmas with new urgency. There was an eagerness to establish a concept of the past not because – as in Britain – a new economic and social order had left people feeling rootless, but because the young country was beginning to acquire a sense of nationhood. America needed traditions and it needed them fast. As far as Christmas was concerned, in its 17th-century colonial past America had reproduced the differences of the opposed sides in England's Civil War: the Cavaliers and Episcopalians in Virginia celebrated in high style, while in New England, there was a five shilling fine to prevent people from doing so. During the 18th century the tradition in America was generally urban, and flourished particularly among merchants, by contrast with the predominantly rural English tradition.

In places where there was co-operation with Native Americans, the season was known as the Big Eating, which is as good a name as any for our modern celebrations. (Curiously, the tradition of the Yule log was tied in with the slavery laws. Slaves' contracts specified that they

ABOVE: *The wild boar head being served for Christmas dinner, engraving from Washington Irving's* Old Christmas

should have seven days' rest around Christmas, or as long as it took the yule log to burn – so they soaked it in water to make it last as long as possible. A water-logged tree trunk was proverbially said to have 'as much water as a Christmas log'.) After 1791, when the Constitution was promulgated, separating Church and State, religious tensions between the communities eased, and Christmas began to be widely celebrated as a binding instrument. Wildly extravagant and imaginative Christmas balls are recorded in the early 1800s in Texas, in Montana and in New Mexico.

But Irving's Olde Worlde view quickly superseded these vigorous native variations, supplying the approved images for a season that became the central point of the commercial and the religious year. *A Christmas Carol* then supplanted the Irving version. Within a year or two of its appearance its sales had outstripped those of the Bible, and Dickens' position as America's favourite foreign-born author was clinched.

***

It was with his visit to America in 1867 – at Christmas time – that Dickens' fame ascended almost to the level of a cult. When he read *A Christmas Carol* in New York, the *Tribune* was moved to say: 'Everyone in the vast assembly was united in wanting to do homage to a man of true and beneficent genius . . . nor in all that great throng was there a single mind unconscious of the privilege it enjoyed in being able, even so partially, to thank Charles Dickens for all the happiness he has given to the world. It is a better world because of him.'

Despite his increasingly poor health – at the New York readings in Steinway Hall the programmes were slipped with a card which read, 'Mr Charles Dickens begs indulgence for a Severe Cold, but hopes its effects may not be very perceptible after a few minutes Reading' – the response of the audience was warm and spontaneous, including, Dickens noted with gratified surprise, clapping 'whenever they laugh or cry'. In Boston 'one poor girl in mourning burst into a passion of grief for Tiny Tim, and was taken out'. Even more gratifyingly, in Vermont a local manufacturer, after hearing Dickens read *A Christmas Carol*, decided for the first time to give his employees Christmas day off, and the following year he gave each of them a turkey.

In order to give these performances, Dickens had rallied remarkably on the night; he was for the most part confined to his quarters, refusing all visits. The poet Henry Wadsworth Longfellow was one of the few people he saw, and the poet discerned a haunted, driven quality in his old friend: he described him as '*fato profugus*', using the phrase by which Virgil denoted Aeneas' flight from his remorseless destiny. On Christmas Day 1867,

ABOVE: *Charles Dickens giving a public reading, painting by James Bacon (fl. 1850)*

Dickens had to travel by train from Boston to New York. He was profoundly depressed. Friends came to cheer him up, offering him seasonal greetings, but they were 'a signal failure, and the kindly wishes ended in a perfect break-down of speech and heart'. When they caught a glimpse of him, his fellow-passengers cheered him; but this only depressed him further.

Even now, though, his sense of humour did not entirely desert him: on another train journey he had a conversation with a small girl who told him that she had read all his novels more than once. When he expressed surprise, she confided in him that she 'sometimes skipped the dull parts – not the short dull parts, but the long dull parts'. Despite a visit to the theatre to see a Sensation Drama, and another to the New York Police Station-House at 3 a.m. to study the faces of condemned murderers (which so fascinated him that he was unable to tear himself away), and a ride in a sleigh through Central Park – about the only seasonal activity he could bear to indulge in – the persistence of his influenza and what he called 'the low action of the heart' kept him in a very subdued frame of mind.

At the last public reading in America, which took place in New York, he of course read *A Christmas Carol*; on medical advice he had to prop up his left foot on a stool. The reading went dazzlingly, and at the end, shaking with emotion, he addressed the audience: 'Ladies and gentlemen, the shadow of one word has impended over me all this evening, and the time has come at last when that shadow must fall . . . ladies and gentlemen, I beg to bid you farewell, and I pray God bless you and God bless the land in which I leave you.'

He returned gladly to England, and to improved health, but only temporarily. The last Christmas of his life, Christmas of 1869, was spent at Gad's Hill, but his foot was so swollen that he could not come down from his room until the evening, finally unable to resist the prospect of party games. At first he just observed, but then, when they played his favourite Memory Game, in which each participant has to recall everything that the person before him has said, adding another phrase, his contribution, after perfectly recalling the whole sequence, was 'Warren's Blacking, 30 the Strand' – the blacking warehouse where he had worked as a child of twelve. He named it with a curious twinkle in his eye, which struck his son Henry forcibly at the time; but the meaning of the words was quite lost on the family, who knew nothing whatever of their father's unhappy childhood. The following day, Boxing Day, he made a speech saying that he hoped that 'we shall do it again next year'; but he was wrong. After yet another gruelling reading tour in January 1870, he 'vanished from these garish lights . . . forever more', returning to Gad's Hill, where he died in June of that year, at the age of fifty-eight.

The festival which Dickens had so unforgettably dramatized grew and grew in the English-speaking world, and its growth was inseparable from his name. It was in his name, too, that people reiterated the demand he had so powerfully made, that in the midst of our own joyful celebrations we should always remember the poor. Nowhere was this true more than in America. In Louisa May Alcott's story 'A Christmas dream and how it came true', published in *Harper's Young People* in 1882, the Scrooge-like heroine – a little girl – re-reads *A Christmas Carol* and is converted to kindness, taking some of her dolls to an orphanage. Shortly after the *Carol*'s first publication in America, the chapter describing the Cratchits' meal was sold as a separate book under the title *Their Christmas Dinner*. Inspired by Dickens' plea that the poor should not go unfed at Christmas, the notion of charitable dinners took hold. They swiftly became perverted by the self-promoting ostentation of the givers; even at the Salvation Army's mass feedings in New York in the late 19th century, where

ABOVE: *'Dear child, you are lost, and I have come to find you', illustration for Louisa May Alcott's*
A Christmas dream and how it came true, *from the cover of* Harper's Young People, *5 December 1882*

up to 25,000 people were given Christmas dinner, the well-off could buy boxes and gallery seats to watch the poor eat. The famous Bowery Christmas dinners spread across the whole area, with special meals for special groups: orphans, Negroes, newsboys. But there was a growing sense of unease about this charitable circus; and it was Dickens, strangely, who got the blame. 'Dickens did more harm than anyone else,' said the *Saturday Evening Post.* 'A great Christmas dinner, in the minds of many, cancels the charity obligations of the entire year.'

A feeling grew that some sort of centralized, anonymous distribution of seasonal charity would be more wholesome. Conceivably; but it would have been anathema to Dickens, to whom the personal element, the generous impulse and its discharge from one human being to another, was the crucial factor. The abolition of the Christmas dinners would have seemed to him another part of the plot of the haves against the have-nots, to deprive them, if not of the food itself, but of their dignity and fun. As Chesterton angrily observed, Scrooge was 'far behind the social reformers of our own day. If he refused to subscribe to the scheme for giving people Christmas dinners, at least he did not subscribe (as the reformers do) to a scheme for taking away the Christmas dinners they have already got. He had no part in the blasphemy of abolishing in work-houses the Christmas ale that had been the charity of Christian people. Doubtless he would have regarded the charity as folly, but he would also have regarded the forcible reversal of it as theft.'

Despite the *Saturday Evening Post*'s denunciation of him, Dickens' indispensability to Christmas continued unchallenged. Norman Rockwell, the Painter Laureate of Middle America, was an enthusiastic and discerning admirer of Dickens. 'I was very deeply impressed and moved by Dickens,' he wrote. 'The variety, the sadness, the happiness, treachery . . .the sharp impressions of dirt, food, inns, horses, streets and people . . .' Accordingly, when he was asked to contribute covers to the Christmas editions of the *Saturday Evening Post*, he decided – ironically, perhaps, in view of the earlier condemnation of his influence – to create Dickensian images, somewhat in contrast to the Washington Irving-inspired ones provided by his friendly competitor J.C. Leydendecker. Norman Rockwell's mostly refer to the Muggleton Stage Coach in *The Pickwick Papers*, also featuring the Fezziwigs, Tiny Tim and Bob Cratchit; they strongly confirmed the identity of Dickens with Christmas.

In the 1930s, as Karal Ann Marling relates, *A Christmas Carol* grew to new levels of fame thanks to the radio, and the annual broadcast on Christmas Day, when Lionel Barrymore would play the role of Scrooge (in full make-up), was a regular fixture for most American families. Marling notes that the broadcast took place at 5 p.m., just when the feast was coming to a close. The Cratchits were central to the broadcast adaptation,and working-class America identified strongly with them; the Depression of the 1930s created an economic background not dissimilar to theirs. President Roosevelt, harbinger of the New Deal, and a politician of whom Dickens might have warmly approved (there were not many of whom that could be said), was known to read *A Christmas Carol* out loud to his family every Christmas Eve; his widow, Eleanor, recorded the story in the 1950s. Part of the extraordinary power of the novel is that it is equally relevant in good times and bad times; its vigorous affirmation of human values, and its denunciation of injustice, are untouched by fashion.

The only images of Christmas that owe nothing to Dickens are those of the Nativity (though in the *Life of Christ* he wrote for his children, he gives a concise and appropriately forthright account of the famous scene) and that curious mutation of Father Christmas, Santa Claus, a Christmas figure in whose evolution Washington Irving was again crucial. In Irving's burlesque, *The History of New York from the Beginning of the World Etc. by Dietrich Knickerbocker* (1809) – a book which Dickens as 'a small and not over-particularly-taken-care-of child' carried in his pocket till it was worn out – he evokes, in a few fleeting references to 'rattling down chimneys' and 'laying his finger beside his nose', Saint Nicholas, the patron saint of the Dutch New Yorkers satirized in the book, and the ur-Santa Claus who would come to supplant Father Christmas as the human embodiment of the festive season. He is clearly a version of the Dutch and German figure of Kriss-Kringle, merged somewhat arbitrarily with Saint Nicklaus, the patron saint of children, and elsewhere known as Pelznichol, Bellschniggle, Bellsnickle.

In 1821, Pelznichol, according to Phyllis Siefker in her entertaining piece of sleuthing, *Santa Claus, Last of the Wild Men*, first appeared as Santeclaus in *The Children's Friend* in the following verse:

Olde SANTECLAUS with much delight
His reindeer drives this frosty night,
O'er chimney tops and tracks of snow,
To bring his yearly gifts to you.

The character was given another evolutionary development in the 1820s by the pedantic and notoriously tetchy professor of linguistics, Clement Clarke Moore, of Boston, Massachusetts, in his still well-known poem *The Night Before Christmas*, in which the whole panoply of reindeer and chimneys and sacks of presents appears for the first time in its fully-fledged version.

It was not, however, until 1862, during the American Civil War, that the twenty-two-year-old German-American illustrator Thomas Nast gave Santa Claus his definitive form. In a pro-Union cartoon called *Santa in Camp*, Santa is shown in a Union Army camp, dressed in the Stars and Stripes, handing our presents. Nast was a polemical cartoonist, and his enlistment of Santa Claus to the Union cause was a masterstroke. Santa became, as the essayist Adam Gopnik notes, 'a Union local deity – a positive spirit of Northern plenty and domesticity, to set alongside and against the Southern myth of chivalry and tradition and deep indigenous culture'. Gopnik contrasts him with Dickens' Spirit of Christmas Present, with whom he shares, as Gopnik says, 'a family resemblance', but Dickens' figure is 'having a good time, not running a good-time business', whereas Santa is 'the model of a Yankee go-getter, Babbitt at the North Pole'. And as such, it is entirely fitting that Santa Claus should have become the Saint of Christmas Consumerism, to be discovered most commonly in those shrines of materialism, large department stores

***

ABOVE: The Legend of St Nicholas, *painting by Gerard David (c. 1460–1523)*
PAGE 156: A Visit from St Nicholas, *a folding book illustrating the poem by Clement Clarke Moore (1779–1863)*
PAGE 157: *An early image of Father Christmas as we know him today, painting by Thomas Nast (1840–1902)*
PAGE 158: *Mr Fezziwig's Ball. An original illustration from* A Christmas Carol, *drawing by John Leech*
PAGE 160: The Return of Sir Christmas, c.*1850*

A VISIT FROM St. NICHOLAS

PUBLISHED BY L. PRANG & Co.
159, WASH.^{TN} ST. BOSTON.

ENTERED ACCORDING TO ACT OF CONGRESS IN THE YEAR 1864, BY
L. PRANG & CO IN THE CLERKS OFFICE OF THE DISTRICT COURT OF MASS.

'Twas the night before Christmas, when all through
the house
Not a creature was stirring, not even a mouse;
The stockings were hung by the chimney with care,
In hopes that St. Nicholas soon would be there;
The children were nestled all snug in their beds,

While visions of sugar-plums danced in their heads;
And mamma in her kerchief and I in my cap,
Had just settled our brains for a long winter's nap,
When out on the lawn there rose such a clatter,
I sprang from my bed to see what was the matter,
Away to the window I flew like a flash,

Tore open the shutters and threw up the sash.
The moon, on the breast of the new-fallen snow,
Gave a lustre of mid-day to objects below;
When, what to my wondering eyes should appear,
But a miniature sleigh, and eight tiny rein-deer,
With a little old driver, so lively and quick,

I knew in a moment it must be St. Nick.
More rapid than eagles his coursers they came,
And he whistled and shouted and called them by name;
"Now, Dasher! now, Dancer! now, Prancer and Vixen!
On! Comet, on! Cupid, on! Dunder and Blitzen,—

To the top of the porch, to the top of the wall!
Now, dash away, dash away, dash away all!"
As dry leaves that before the wild hurricane fly,
When they meet with an obstacle, mount to the sky,
So, up to the house-top the coursers they flew,
With a sleigh full of toys—and St. Nicholas too.

And then in a twinkling I heard on the roof,
The prancing and pawing of each little hoof.
As I drew in my head, and was turning around,
Down the chimney St. Nicholas came with a bound.
He was dressed all in fur from his head to his foot,

And his clothes were all tarnished with ashes and soot;
A bundle of toys he had flung on his back,
And he looked like a pedler just opening his pack.
His eyes how they twinkled! his dimples how merry!
His cheeks were like roses, his nose like a cherry;
His droll little mouth was drawn up like a bow,

And the beard on his chin was as white as the snow;
The stump of a pipe he held tight in his teeth,
And the smoke, it encircled his head like a wreath.
He had a broad face and a little round belly
That shook when he laughed, like a bowl full of jelly.

He was chubby and plump,—a right jolly old elf;
And I laughed when I saw him in spite of myself.
A wink of his eye, and a twist of his head,
Soon gave me to know I had nothing to dread.
He spoke not a word, but went straight to his work,
And filled all the stockings; then turned with a jerk,

And laying his finger aside of his nose,
And giving a nod, up the chimney he rose.
He sprang to his sleigh, to his team gave a whistle,
And away they all flew like the down of a thistle.
But I heard him exclaim, ere he drove out of sight,
"MERRY CHRISTMAS TO ALL, AND TO ALL A GOOD NIGHT!"

MERRY CHRISTMAS TO ALL AND TO ALL A GOOD NIGHT

Despite having been marketed and plagiarized and vulgarized in a million different ways in the hundred and fifty years since it was written, *A Christmas Carol* – the supreme embodiment of what Dickens called his 'carol philosophy' – 'cheerful views, sharp anatomization of humbug, jolly good temper; papers always in season, pat to the time of year; and a vein of glowing, hearty, generous, mirthful, beaming reference in everything to Home, and Fireside' – Dickens' Christmas, in fact – remains as potent a definition as ever of an aspect of the human condition, its images and its messages still profoundly affecting and necessary. Dickens has made sure that, however vacuous Christmas may have become, at some point or another we all ask ourselves about those who have no place at the feast. Whether we do anything about it or not, is, of course, up to us.

BIBLIOGRAPHY

The Annotated Christmas Carol, M.P. Hearn (Clarkson N. Potter, 1976)

The Art and Politics of Thomas Nast, Morton Keller (O.U.P. 1968)

A Celebration of Christmas, ed. Gillian Cooke (Queen Anne Press, 1980)

Charles Dickens and the Stage, Thomas E. Pemberton (G. Redway,1888)

Charles Dickens, G.K. Chesterton (Methuen & Co., 1906)

Charles Dickens, Peter Ackroyd (Sinclair-Stevenson, 1990)

Christmas: A Social History, Mark Connelly (I.B. Tauris, 1999)

The Christmas Card, George Buday (Rockliff, 1954)

A Christmas Carol and Other Tales, intro. by G.K. Chesterton (Waverley Editions, 1913)

Christmas Fare, Judith Hold and Alison Harding (Webb & Bower, 1981)

Christmas Past, Gavin Weightman and Steve Humphries (Sidgwick & Jackson, 1987)

The Christmas Reader: A Treasury of Christmas Verse and Prose, ed. Godfrey Smith (Viking, 1985)

Dickens of London, Wolf Mankowitz (Weidenfeld and Nicolson, 1976)

Dickens the Dramatist, F. Dubrez Fawcett (W.H. Allen, 1952)

Drinking with Dickens, Cedric Dickens (Elvendon, 1983)

The Pilgrim Edition of the Letters of Charles Dickens, ed. Graham Storey et al. (O.U.P. 2002)

The Life of Charles Dickens, John Forster (Chapman and Hall, 1874)

The Making of the Modern Christmas, J.M. Golby and A.W. Purdue (Batsford, 1986)

Merry Christmas! Celebrating America's Greatest Holiday, Karal Ann Marling (Harvard University Press, 2000)

Mr and Mrs Charles Dickens Entertain at Home, Helen Cox (Pergamon,1970)

Oxford Reader's Companion to Dickens, Paul Schlicke (O.U.P. 1999)

Santa Claus, The Last of the Wild Men, Phyllis Siefker (McFarland & Company, 1997)

Thomas Nast's Christmas Drawings, Intro. by Thomas Nast St Hill (Dover Publications, 1979)

A Treasury of Christmas, Frank & Jamie Muir (Robson Books, 1981)

The Victorian Christmas Book, Antony and Peter Miall (Dent, 1978)

The Winter Solstice: The Sacred Traditions of Christmas, John Matthews (Godsfield Press and Thorsons, 1998)

The World of Charles Dickens, Angus Wilson (Martin-Secker and Warburg, 1970)

The World of Charles Dickens (Pitkin Guides, 1999)

ACKNOWLEDGMENTS

The Publishers have made every effort to contact holders of copyright works. Any copyright holders we have been unable to reach are invited to contact the Publishers so that a full acknowledgment may be given in subsequent editions. For permission to reproduce the images on the following pages and for supplying photographs, the Publishers thank those listed below.

AKG, London: 20 (British Library), 34, 139 (Volkskundehaus, Ried), 144–5, 158

AKG, London/Erich Lessing: 19 (The Louvre, Paris)

Courtesy Louisa May Alcott Memorial Foundation, Orchard House, Concord, MA: 152

The Art Archive: 2, 6–7 (Alfred Dunhill Collection/Eileen Tweedy), 35, 42–3, 132 (Eileen Tweedy),
    133 (Eileen Tweedy), 147, 148

Bridgeman Art Library: 3 (Dickens House Museum, London), 11 (Dickens House Museum, London),
    14–15 (Palazzo Vecchio, Florence), 16 (British Library), 31 (Illustrated London News Picture Library,
    London), 36–7 (Dickens House Museum, London), 40 (Dickens House Museum, London),
    112–3 (Private Collection), 120 (Private Collection), 121 (Fitzwilliam Museum, University of
    Cambridge), 126 (Private Collection), 134 (Dickens House Museum, London), 135 (Mallett & Son
    Antiques Limited, London), 136 (Stapleton Collection), 137 below (Private Collection), 138 (City of
    Westminster Archive Centre, London), 141 (Illustrated London News Picture Library, London), 150
    (Eastgate Museum, Rochester), 155 (National Gallery of Scotland, Edinburgh), 160 (Private Collection)

© Christie's Images Limited, 2003: 116–117

Getty Images: 10

The Metropolitan Museum of Art: 124–5 (gift of Mr and Mrs Stephen Whitney Blodgett, 1983
    [1983.486], photograph © 1984 The Metropolitan Museum of Art)

Private collections: 1, 12, 13, 22, 23, 39, 41, 44, 115, 119, 123, 129, 131, 156, 157

By courtesy of Sotheby's Picture Library, London: endpapers, 25, 28–9, 32–3

Tate, London (2003); on loan to the National Portrait Gallery, London: 4

V&A Picture Library: 137 above